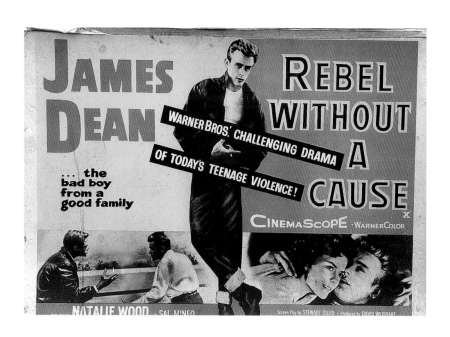

HOT ROD
MEMORABILIA & COLLECTIBLES

David Fetherston

Motorbooks International
Publishers & Wholesalers

DEDICATION

To my friend Pete Pesterre,
Editor of *Popular Hot Rodding Magazine*, family man, drag racer, car builder, photographer, writer,
and all-around good guy, killed accidentally in 1992 doing what he liked best—driving flat out.

First published in 1996 by Motorbooks International Publishers & Wholesalers, 729 Prospect Avenue, PO Box 1, Osceola, WI 54020-0001

Library of Congress Cataloging-in-Publication Data
Fetherston, David A.
   Hot rod memorabilia & collectibles / David A. Fetherston.
      p.   cm.
   Includes index.
   ISBN 0-7603-0131-X (pbk.)
   1. Hot rods—Collectibles.   I. Title.
TL236.3.F4723 1996
629.228—dc20   96-21031

On the Front Cover: The variety hot rod collectibles and memorabilia is endless—from toy and model cars, decals from performance parts suppliers, patches and programs from famous hot rod events, to books, magazines, movie posters, and more.
On the Frontispiece: One of the most popular movie posters is from *Rebel Without a Cause*. An original is rare and expensive, but reproductions are available.
On the Title Pages: Three of the many popular and collectible Hot Wheels toy cars: the '32 Vicky and the '36 Ford coupe, both issued in 1969, and *Sir Rodney Roadster*, issued in 1974.
On the Back Cover: More of the infinite variety of hot rod collectibles: the boxes from model car kits, record album covers, and Ed Roth's *Rat Fink Comix*.

Printed in Hong Kong

CONTENTS

ACKNOWLEDGMENTS

The hobby of hot rodding has a rich cultural history. It has emerged from an activity deemed socially unacceptable to one of America's most fascinating motorsports. It is enjoyed by a wide collection of ethnic and socially diverse auto enthusiasts. This book attempts to capture an overview of the toys, literature, clothing, and art that have become a premier field for collectors of Americana.

The following people graciously allowed me to photograph their collections of hot rod memorabilia: "Barefoot" Gary, George Barris, Don Bishop, Steve Castelli, Ed Hagerty, Chico Komada, John LaBelle, Rod Powell, Greg Sharp, Greg Williams, Mich Silver, Shige Suganuma, Vern Tardell, John Thompson from Thompson's Auto Literature, and Tony Thacker. I would also like to thank Richard Oakley for his help with hot rod comics, Johnny "Big Hand" Bartlett for his help and advice with hot rod records, and Ron Main from "Main Attraction" movie memorabilia in Canoga Park, California, for his help and advice on hot rod movie posters.

At Fetherston Publishing, I thank Gloria Fetherston and Nanette Simmons for taking care of the editing and production details.

David Fetherston

INTRODUCTION

The first time I rolled my toy cars across the floor I was hooked on horsepower, and when I saw my first hot rod, I fell in love. The raw essence of power and lawlessness hot rods exuded in the 1950s made the hair on the back of my neck rev' up. There were few hot rod toys available to me at the time or I'm sure I would have headed for them. Over the years I became a collector of car "stuff" and have become particularly interested in land speed and Bonneville cars.

For this book I have assembled a diverse selection of collectibles: clothing, toys, records, movie souvenirs, books, and vintage magazines. The width and breadth of collecting hot rod related memorabilia is enormous and some of the collections I have visited are mind-boggling. Many collectors focus on one subject only, such as vintage magazine first issues of *Honk*, *Hot Rod*, *American Rodder*, and *Rodding and Restyling*. Others select club jackets and club plaques as their specialty.

I have attempted to give readers a good taste of hot rod collectibles and have included a generalized pricing guide for them. The prices quoted have been gathered from many sources and from personal experience. I believe that value is at the discretion of the seller and at the whim of the buyer and no value guide beyond that is offered. Great sources for more material on this hobby for hot rod collectors can be found in Sue Elliott's new monthly magazine *Car Toys*, in *Mobilia* magazine, and in the annual *Goodguys Gazette Collectors Issue.*

Hot rod toys today are sizzling hot for collectors. They are so hot that even new hot rod toy releases of the Plymouth Prowler are being snapped up immediately. Collecting hot rod toys is not as costly as other toy collecting because hot rod toys are of mostly mass-produced post-war vintage. The new collectibles are marketed as "art" and have artistic pricing.

Hot rod toys vary in size from 1-inch-long tiny pot metal Tootsietoys to stamped metal land speed cars from Kingsbury, which are up to 24 inches in length. Fabrication methods for these toys includes molded or injected plastic, tin litho, wood, fiberglass, and cast white metal.

The earliest hot rod toys are the land speed record cars from Kingsbury and Ranlite. Kingsbury, originally from Keene, New Hampshire, created a set of four land speed cars in the late 1920s and early 1930s. They were two different vintage Malcolm Campbell Blue-birds, the Henry Segrave 1,000-horse-power Sunbeam and the Golden Arrow.

Many small toy companies flowered during this time and it was these manufacturers who first built hot rod toys. Nosco Plastics from Erie, Pennsylvania, created two hot rod toys in the early 1950s, the Hot 'See *"Hopped-Up" Hot Rod* with a four-cylinder see-through engine and working pistons driven through a gear mounted on the front axle and a similar V-8-powered *Vizy Vee Stockcar* was also offered.

During this time two small manufacturers turned out some nicely realistic hot rod roadsters. Renwal from New York City and Saunders Tool & Die Co. from Aurora, Illinois, created a line of toys which included

T-N: Ford hot rod roadster, *Dream Boat*, 10 inch, tin, Japan, friction drive, sparking engine, circa 1960.

Top Right
Collection of pot metal hot rods from Tootsietoy, Midget, and an unknown Hong Kong manufacturer. 1 inch approx. Manufactured as dime store toys from after the 1930s until the mid-1960s. Some still in production.

Bottom Right
Auburn Rubber: Three set hot rod roadsters, 4 inch, chrome painted engine/trunk lid, one piece rubber molded, plastic wheels, circa 1950.

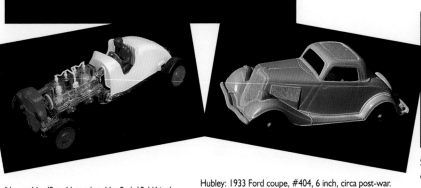

Saunders: Hot rod, 7 inch, molded red plastic, friction drive, circa 1950.

Hubley: 1933 Ford coupe, #404, 6 inch, circa post-war.

Nosco: Hot 'See, *Hopped-up Hot Rod*, 10 1/4 inch, plastic, friction drive, circa 1950.

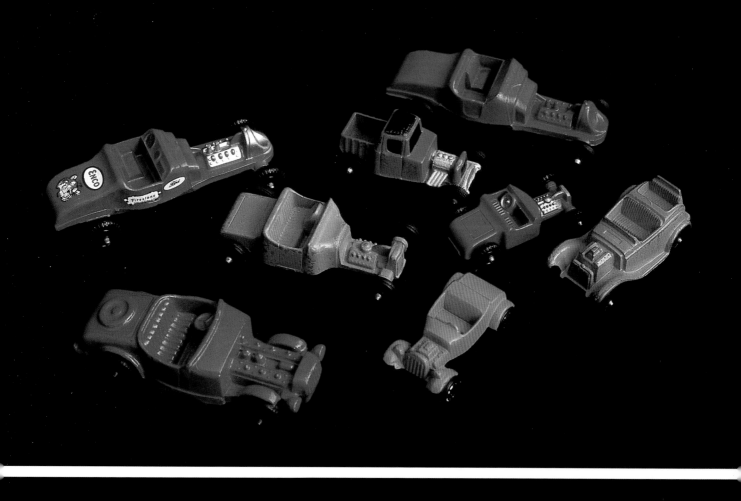

MS Toys: *Prop-Rod*, 10 inch, tin litho, friction drive, circa 1955.

hot rods. Saunders followed Nosco Plastics with a roadster and stock car with friction engines. Molded in plastic, the Saunders '34 Ford roadster was cute and well scaled. The Renwal roadster also featured an open engine and a driver but it was less detailed, and while the body resembled a '32, the grille was generic.

Another line of little hot rod toys that are often overlooked came from Tootsietoy. Tootsietoys were issued in two scales in the early 1950s, 3-inch and 6-inch. The first hot rod Tootsietoy was a '31 Ford B hot rod which came in the 3-inch scale and was followed by a 1940 Ford V-8 hot rod in the 6-inch scale. They were made in white metal with plastic tires and crimped steel axles. Other manufacturers created imaginary land speed cars in the smaller scale including Barclay, Hubley, Best, and Britains.

The Revell Toy Company was started in 1951 by Lewis Glaser in Venice, California, with a series of auto toys including a *Backfiring Hot Rod,* which had toy pistol caps inside the bodywork and could be triggered remotely. Revell's first traditional hot rod was a 3/4-inch scale kit of only 11 pieces, which sold for 79¢.

Japanese tin toy makers, such as T-N Company, MS Toys, and Alps Company did a few friction-engined or roll-along hot rods, including roadsters such as the T-N Company's *The Bug* and the Alps Company's *Rainbow T-Bucket. The Bug* from the mid-1950s featured flip up and down rockers on the engine and flamed red bodywork. Early tin hot rods were all metal, but by the mid-1960s, Japanese toys like the *Rainbow T-Bucket* were made of plastic and litho tin.

By the early 1970s American toy makers, including Aurora, which had traditionally sold plastic kits, introduced action toys. Their "Impostors" series had a clockwork engine which transformed a 1940 Willys coupe into a stretched funny car as it ran across the ground. Another action toy used flywheel power with a toothed pull-start.

During the 1970s small plastic toys became popular and cheap. Both Hasbro and Ideal produced hot rod toys of a woody and a roadster. Hot rod toys designed to go in the sandbox came from Buddy L and Nylint. Both companies offered cool toys including Buddy L's *Ol'Buddy's Custom Surf-N-Dump,* and Nylint's *Hot Rod Roadster, Pickup,* and *Rumble Seat T.*

In the 1990s, hot rod toys have been made by a dozen different makers from Japan, Taiwan, Thailand and the United States, and can be found in local drugstores or toy stores. Other more modern, hot rod toy collecting involves new collectibles. Pieces like the *Moonliner* by Jocko Johnson, the *Piersen Coupe* by Steve Possen, and the *So-Cal Tank* from Bret Banker's AutoDeco are popular but expensive.

Prices for these toys vary enormously. "Used and enjoyed" obviously price differently to "boxed and mint." Kingsbury land speed cars from the 1930s go from $300 to $1,200. Sandbox toys from Buddy L and Nylint are $20 to $150. Renwal, Saunders and Nosco Plastics toys run from $25 to $120. Tootsietoy: Both scales price at $2 to $40. A new one is $3.99. Japanese tin toys from T-N Company, MS Toy, and Alps, etc., vary widely—1950s: $200 to $400; 1960s: $100 to $250; later: $20 and up. Aurora 1970s action toys range from $5 to $40. Small plastic cars from Hasbro and Ideal are $5 to $15. Collectible hot rods and land speed cars price at $120 to $600 and up.

Manufacturer unknown: Ford hot rod roadster, 10 inch, tin litho, Japan, friction drive, circa 1958.

T-N: Ford hot rod roadster, *The Bug*, 10 inch, tin litho, Japan, friction drive, moving engine rockers, circa 1958.

This 1974 Matchbox street rod, #K50 *Hot T* is a rare 1/43rd model from this British manufacturer.

Ford hot rod T-bucket, 12 inch, tin litho and plastic, Japan, friction drive, see-through engine. 1965.

Process Plastic: Three set hot rod roadsters, 5 inch, chrome engines, folding windscreen frames, plastic injection molded, circa 1964.

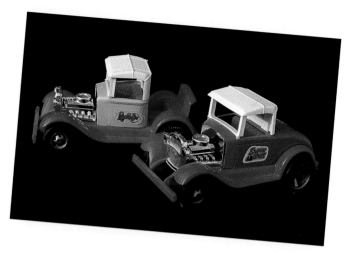

Tonka: Ford hot rod roadsters, 4 inch, chrome engines, multiple injection molded parts, circa 1978.

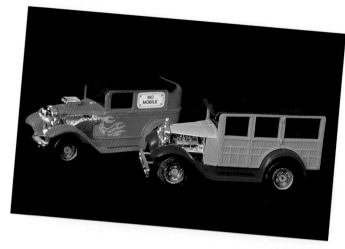

Ideal Toy: 1929 Ford woodie and sedan delivery, 2 inch, chrome engines, multiple injection molded parts, friction drive, circa 1978.

Tootsietoy: 1940 Ford roadster, 4 inch, cast metal and plastic, free wheeling, circa 1988.

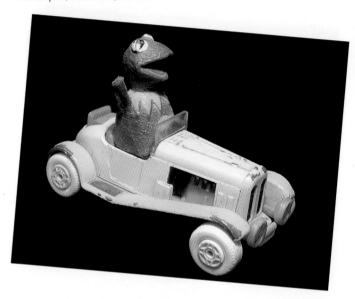

Corgi Toys: *Kermit the Frog Hot Rod*, 3 1/2 inch, cast metal and plastic, free wheeling, circa 1979.

Tootsietoy: 1940 Willys hot rod, 4 inch, cast metal and plastic, free wheeling, circa 1990.

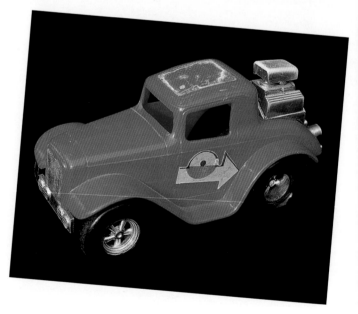

Hasbro: Hot rod coupe, 5 inch, injected plastic and metal, flywheel-powered, circa 1978.

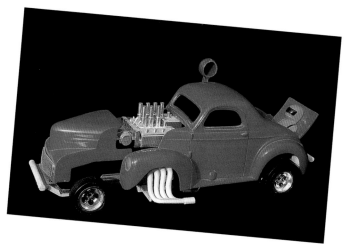

Aurora: Imposters series, 1940 Willys coupe/funny car, 9 1/2 inch, injected plastic and metal, 1972.

Corgi Toys: Wizz Wheels series, Jag-powered Austin, 2 1/2 inch, metal and plastic, free wheeling, circa 1982.

Nylint: Hot rod collection, 10 inch, pressed metal and plastic, free wheeling red 1929 Ford Pick-up; yellow 1929 Ford roadster; blue 1932 Ford Truck roadster.

Buddy L: 1932 Ford roadster, 10 inch, pressed metal and plastic, free wheeling, circa 1985.

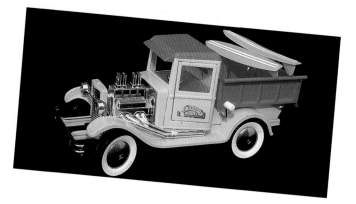

Buddy L: *Ol' Buddy's Custom Surf-N-Dump*, 10 inch, pressed metal and plastic, free wheeling, circa 1970.

Manufacturer unknown: 1932 hot rod roadster, slot car, 3 inch, plastic and metal, electric powered, circa 1960.

Manufacturer unknown: Chopped 1932 Ford hot rod, slot car, 3 inch, plastic and metal, electric powered, circa 1968.

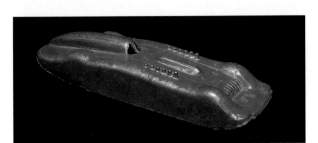

Midgetoy: *LSR Racer*, 3 1/2 inch, cast metal, free wheeling, circa 1960.

Lledo: 1935 *Blue Bird LSR*, Kelloggs Land Speed Legends promotional, 4 1/2 inch, cast metal and plastic, free wheeling, 1990.

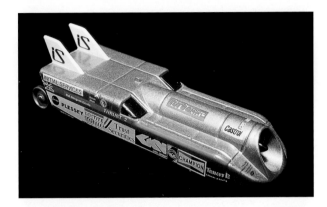

Lledo: 1983 *Thrust 2 LSR*, Kelloggs Land Speed Legends promotional, 4 1/2 inch, cast metal and plastic, free wheeling, 1990.

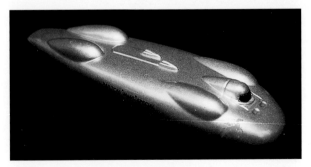

Lledo: 1947 *Railton Mobile Special LSR*, Kelloggs Land Speed Legends promotional, 4 1/2 inch, cast metal and plastic, free wheeling, 1990.

Kingsbury: *Golden Arrow Racer*, 20 inch, pressed metal, wind-up motor, circa 1935.

₂ TETHER CARS

Few hot rod toys were powered except for some tin and plastic toys which needed a push to get them going for a few feet, via a friction-drive engine. However, there was a small group of scale car racers who loved to play in a circle with miniature versions of real hot rods powered by internal combustion engines. These were, and in some case still are, the tether car racers or "spindizzies."

These racers parallel the control line model airplane flyers using similar single-cylinder gas engines and controlling their toys by wire. Tether cars like the *All American Hot Rod* came with a hand-held "tether" so the car could be raced as either a "whip car" or gas-powered on an open section of paving; however, at this point the similarity to model airplane flying stops. In general, dedicated tether car racers ran them on a circular track "tethered" off a center pole via a fine long wire.

On the tether, only one car raced at a time against the clock but racers had a second variation which modified the car to run on a rail track, putting up to four cars in direct competition.

Tether cars date from the mid-1930s. At about that time Ray Snow, a model airplane hobbyist, created a small gas-powered car using one of his airplane engines. From this point on, the sport grew in intensity. At first, speeds of 20 miles per hour were considered fast but they rapidly increased to 40, 80, and 100 miles per hour.

These cars initially resembled speedway or Indy roadsters but they soon evolved into hot rods or gas coupes from the dry lakes. Not surprisingly, some of these cars evolved just as dry lakes racing was becoming popular.

Two scales of cars appeared, mite cars and full-size cars. The mite cars were only 10 to 12 inches long and were powered by tiny .029 ci to .049 ci engines. The larger full-size tether cars were 14 to 20 inches and were powered by considerably larger and faster .060 ci engines. Popular mite models for collectors include Thimble Drome/Cox, McCoy, and Cameron. Highly collectible full-size brands include Dooling, Korn, Gardner-Welsh, Richter, Bremer, Hurricane, and Whirlwind.

Tether car racing peaked just after World War II and rolled downhill after the mid-1950s. By this stage the speed of these cars was approaching 130 miles per hour, but interest was slipping. The rail tracks disappeared first. The tether tracks faded but not as rapidly; they didn't require the upkeep of the wooden rail tracks. Today, only two active tether tracks remain, one in Anderson,

All American Company: *All American Hot Rod*, 9 inch, cast aluminum, gas powered, silver and red. Came with a "tether" for single-handed racing on a wire, either for whip racing or gas powered, 1949.

Cameron Precision Engineering: *Rodzy*, 8 inch, cast aluminum, gas powered, yellow, 1954.

Duro-Matic Products Co.: Muroc Dry Lakes roadster AV-8, 12 inch, cast and polished aluminum, gas-powered Hornet "60-A," unrestored, circa 1948.

All American Company: *All American Hot Rod*, 9 inch long, 5 inch wide, cast aluminum, gas powered, black, 1949. Marketed by Spot Enterprises in Culver City, California, for $3.95 and sold in assorted colors.

Indiana, and the other in the Whittier Narrows, a county recreational park in South El Monte, California.

During their peak in the 1940s and early 1950s, special engines were developed for the mite scale and the full-sized cars including the McCoy 60 Redhead, Dennymite, and the Dooling.

Collecting tether cars was not considered mainstream until the 1980s, when they took off like a spindizzy gone mad. In the early 1980s cars changed hands from $20 for mite-cars to perhaps $1,000 for full-sized cars. If you add one zero, or a couple of zeros, to those figures you have a starting place for pricing today.

The basic reason for this enormous pricing growth is that demand has outstripped supply. Thimble Drome mite cars were the most numerous as they were produced in large numbers and even used as paperboy giveaways for selling subscriptions. However, some of the full-sized cars were built in numbers as low as 5, 10, 30, or maybe even 100 units.

The tether cars, which were scaled hot rods, are just as famous as the big-time speedway tether car names. In 1941 Cal-Lieb introduced a '32 roadster which looked rather blocky but in 1947 McCoy introduced the now-famous *McCoy Hot Rod* and *Roadrunner* tether cars. These roughly scaled '30 Ford roadsters were manufactured in Hollywood by the Duro-Matic Products Company. Made in two sections with the bellypan forming the chassis, they featured a rear gear drive off a horizontally mounted engine.

The Cameron Precision Engineering *Rodzy*, originally built in Chino, California, and then later in Sonora, is the most celebrated tether rod. Thousands of *Rodzys* were wrapped in plain brown paper, boxed, and then shipped with red *Rodzy* artwork. *Rodzys* were sold either as engine-less "pushers" or with a stock .09 ci gas engine and painted black, with the idea that the owner would paint the car anyway.

Today, there is a community of small manufacturers and hobbyists still involved in this sport, building amazingly detailed tether cars for collectors, who will only display the cars. Other manufacturers are replicating old cars or creating parts for the older kits or even creating new hot rod tether cars.

Fryco Engineering in Fullerton, California, and other companies are building tether car streamliners which are ready-to-run race cars. On the Whittier Narrows track, Fryco cars have exceeded 200 miles per hour.

Printed material is rare. Books include *Model Gasoline Engines* by Raymond Yates. A great new book on the subject is *Vintage Miniature Racing Cars* by Bob Ames. *Rail and Cable News* magazine from the late post-war years is excellent and ultra rare.

Pricing of these cars is extremely difficult. Complete mite cars run $350 and up, while full-size cars can price at $1,000 to $10,000; some extremely rare cars change hands at $25,000. The *Rodzy*, which is the most prevalent of all tether cars, sold for $19.95 in 1963 but today will bring up to $500 for a mint boxed version wrapped in brown paper. Swap meet prices start at about $80 and move up.

McCoy Roadrunner: 1932 Ford highboy roadster, 12 inch, cast aluminum, gas powered, circa 1950, restored 1994.

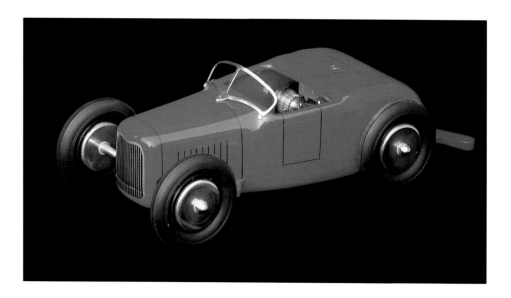

Dooling Frog Streamliner: Dry Lakes' style streamlined coupe, cast aluminum, gas powered, 14 inch, unrestored original car, circa 1947.

Duro-Matic Products Co.: Muroc Dry Lakes roadster AV-8, 12 inch, cast aluminum, gas powered, black, unrestored, circa 1952.

Duro-Matic Products Co.: Muroc Dry Lakes roadster AV-8, 12 inch, cast aluminum, gas powered, blue and silver, unrestored, circa 1952.

McCoy: 1932 Ford highboy roadster, 12 inch, cast aluminum, gas powered, circa 1952, restored 1994.

Cameron Precision Engineering: *Rodzy*, 8 inch, cast aluminum, gas powered, black, mint, box, 1954.

Hornet 60-A Gas Motor advertisement, circa 1952.

Cameron Precision Engineering: *Rodzy*, advertisement, 1954.

Duro-Matic advertisement, 1951.

Roy Richter-Streamliner advertisement, circa 1941.

MODEL KITS

3

There are two schools of thought on the correct way to collect model kits: unassembled and assembled. The collector of unassembled kits displays them for their great box art although it may still contain a complete kit. Other collectors build the kits and then display them on shelves or in showcases, or they may make up a display diorama. This collecting is diversified even more with some collectors specializing in early AMT, Aurora, Pyro, Monogram or specialized kits such as those of Ed Roth.

The earliest hot rod kits were for modelers proficient in wood carving and some of these unassembled kits can still be found. For example, the *Airflo JV8*, a '32 Ford roadster kit made by Airflo in San Bernardino, California, in the late 1940s and 1950s came with eight pieces of preshaped balsa wood, dowel axles, turned wooden wheels, and headlights and a small sheet of decals. The rest was left up to the builder's talent as a wood carver. This style of kit is still marketed and is used by organizations like the Boy Scouts for hobby activities, and many completed wooden roadsters can be found at swap meets.

In the early 1950s, several companies entered the plastic toy kit business and began releasing plastic assembly kits for many types of automobiles. Kits for hot rods followed. Monogram, Aurora, Lindberg, and Revell were all early players.

At first, scales were noted in several ways. One example is the 3/4-inch which indicated a scale of three quarters of an inch to a foot. This was then standardized to sizes including 1/32 scale. Later, standard scale sizes rose to 1/25 and to 1/24 and even in 1964 to a giant 1/8 for the Lindberg *Bobtail T.* Monogram's *Big T* also appeared in 1964 followed by the *Big Deuce*, the *Highboy*, *The Big Tub*, the *Show-Go-Phaeton*, and others.

The early kits are primitive by comparison with some complete kits having as few as 11 components.

Pyro Plastics: Table Top series, *Rebel* and *Jersey Bounce*, 1/32 scale, injected molded plastic, originally priced at 50¢, circa 1962.

Revell: double car kit, *Sanitary "T" bucket* and *Mooneyes dragster*, 1/25 scale, colored injected molded plastic and chromed injected molded plastic, circa 1962.

Ungar: Hot rod kit: 6 inch, snap assembly, electric powered, plastic and metal, circa 1955.

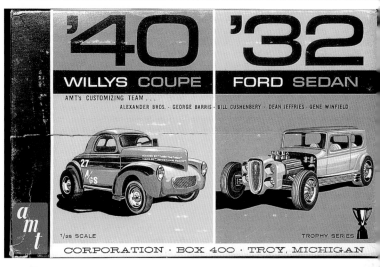

Top
Revell Hot Rod: Hot rod, 3/4-inch scale, injected plastic, free wheeling, Revell's first
hot rod kit, circa 1955.

Middle
Monogram Mattel: *Boss A Bone*, '29 Ford roadster pickup, 1/24 scale, injected molded
plastic and chromed injected molded plastic, circa 1978.

Bottom
Monogram: P-2 hot rod Plastikit, 3/4-inch scale, injected plastic, free wheeling,
assembled, part painted, 1954. Monogram's first hot rod kit.

Top
Airflo: *JV8*, hot rod racer, 5 inch, balsa wood carving kit, free wheeling, 1950.

Middle
AMT: Trophy series double kit, 1940 Willys coupe, 1932 Ford sedan, 1/25 scale,
injected molded plastic and chromed injected molded plastic, circa 1974.

Bottom
Manufacturer unknown: Hand-carved 1932 Ford roadster from wood kit, black, circa 1960.

Left: Monogram advertisement for the *Big Deuce*, 1963. Right: Revell advertisement for 1/25 scale street rods, Ed Roth's *Outlaw* re-issued as *Canned Heat*, 1973.

AMT: Trophy series 3 in 1 Ford kits, the first AMT 1/25 scale series, 1932 Ford Model "B" coupe, 1940 Ford coupe, 1939/40 Ford sedan, 1/25 scale, colored injected molded plastic and chromed injected molded plastic, circa 1959.

Early molding techniques did not allow for complex shapes, and bodies were often formed in 3 pieces. The quality of the styrene plastics of 40 years ago was not very stable, and today, parts may be brittle or warped.

In 1958, the first 1/25 scale kits appeared when AMT introduced its first street rod kit with a hot rodded '32 roadster followed by their Trophy Series in 1959. This line-up eventually expanded to include the now-famous 3-in-1 street rod kits. About this time, Monogram and Aurora also entered the marketplace with their less expensive 1/32 scale kits, increasing the number of parts and adding chrome trim. Monogram kits included the *Black Widow*, a 1927 T pickup, and the *Green Hornet*, a racing roadster.

Box art also improved dramatically with a painted image of the assembled kit taken directly from an existing hot rod. Aurora swiped the design of Clarence Catallo's *Little Deuce Coupe*, which had been built at the Alexander Brothers shop in Detroit, Michigan, and at the Barris shop in California, and reproduced it as the *Ram Rod*. This became their first 49¢ 1/34 series in 1962. Other famous rods were also misappropriated by Aurora including Dave Stuckey's '32 Tudor as the *'32 Skid-Doo* and Joe Cruce's *Tall T* as the *T for Two*. Monogram had their own line of 1/34th scale with "The Forty Niner" series.

The 1960s brought an expanding interest in its, and the variety of offerings exploded with AMT, IMC, and MPC entering the market with Detroit's new cars, hot rods and customs, trucks, and movie cars.

George Barris had models of his customs and hot rods on the market including *Ala Kart* and published a small magazine on model car building called *Model Kars* featuring the AMT 3-in-1 Styline kits. Other magazines, including *Car Modeler* and *Model Car Science*, were dedicated to the hobby while *Car Craft*, *Hot Rod*, and *Rod & Custom* added model car columns.

Revell's kits of Ed "Big Daddy" Roth's wild hot rods took the market by storm; *Tweetie Pie*, *Beatnik Bandit*, *Outlaw*, *Mysterion*, and *Surfite* were all popular kits in their day, and today, original kits command sky-high prices. Other Roth kits were a series of 1/25 scale cartoon characters including *Rat Fink* and *Drag Nut*. Ed Roth and his monster kits expanded into *Brother Rat Fink*, *Surf Fink*, and the *Mr. Gasser* series, which put *Rat Fink* at the helm of hot rods and racing cars.

Metal kits appeared in the mid-1960s from Hubley, which issued a '32 Ford powered by an Offy twin-cam engine. Finer detailed plastic kits came on the market including Monogram's gorgeous rendition of *Li'l Coffin* in 1964 and a 1929 Model A pickup which has been reissued numerous times over the past 30 years with titles such as the *Blue Beetle* and the *Boss A Bone*.

Interest slackened in kits in the late 1960s and continued its downward spiral until the late 1970s. Hot rod kits during this time contained the AMT *Car Craft Dream Rod* designed by Bill Cushenbery and the MPC kit of John Milner's '32 coupe from *American Graffiti*.

There has been a huge resurgence of interest in kits since the mid-1980s with the issuing of new and old kits from established manufacturers and new small companies like Jimmy Flintstone Productions, which makes resin-cast hot rods and custom kits.

Collectors' pricing of kits is remarkable; an unassembled Ed Roth *Surfite* kit recently had an asking price of $1,500. Early wooden 30¢ kits may sell for $20 to $100. Special-interest 1950s kits run $300 to $600, while common kits range from $50 to $125. Rarer 1960s kits run in the $150 to $400 price range, 1970s and 1980s kits can be purchased from $15 to $300. The Giant Ts and '32s run from $80 to $250. Built-up kits in general are not so valuable but can command up to $150. Many early kits are being "re-popped" in limited numbers, much to some collectors' chagrin but it has put some unobtainable kits back on the market in the $10 to $125 range.

Aurora: 1932 Ford custom coupe, *Ram Rod*, replica of Clarence Catallo's famous coupe, 1/32 scale, injected molded plastic, circa 1962.

Lindberg: 1929 Ford roadster, Lindberg Line series, 5 inch, injected molded plastic, circa 1958.

Monogram: Forty Niner series, Ford "T" hot rod, *the Pick-Up*, 5 inch, injected molded plastic, circa 1962.

AMT: Trophy series 3 in 1 Kit, 1934 Ford pickup customizing kit, 1/25 scale, injected molded plastic, circa 1960.

Revell: Highway Pioneers, V-8 hot rod, 1932 Ford, U.S. Modern Series, 5 inch, injected molded plastic, circa 1954.

Aurora: 1927 Ford T pick-up roadster, *The Shiftin Drifter*, 5 inch, injected molded plastic, circa 1962.

This rare Palmer Plastics Inc. 1/32 scale kit sold for 29¢ and was one of three models which this Brooklyn, New York, company issued around 1960.

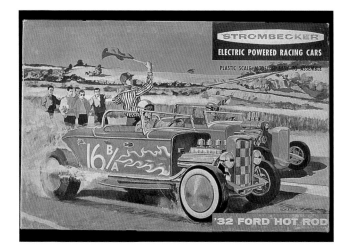

This rare and unusual Strombecker '32 Ford hot rod kit was electric powered and built at 1/24 scale. This Moline, Illinois, company issued only a few hot rod kits, specializing mostly in sports cars.

Monogram: *Big Deuce*, 1932 full-fendered highboy roadster, red and white, 1/8 scale, colored injected molded plastic and chromed injected molded plastic, 1963.

Monogram: *Big Drag*, '27 Ford T roadster, blue, 1/8 scale, colored injected molded plastic and chromed injected molded plastic, 1964.

Monogram: The Big Tub '27 Ford T convertible sedan, 1/8 scale, colored injected molded plastic and chromed injected molded plastic, circa 1965.

Monogram: *Big Deuce*, 1932 highboy roadster, yellow and white, 1/8 scale, colored injected molded plastic and chromed injected molded plastic, circa 1965.

Hubley: Hot rod roadster, assembled with yellow paint finish, 1/25 scale, cast metal and plastic kit, Offy motor, circa 1964.

Monogram: '27 Ford street T roadster pickup, 1/8 scale, colored injected molded plastic and chromed injected molded plastic, 1964.

AMT: *Invader* twin-engined Oakland show-winning red roadster, 1/25 scale, colored injected molded plastic and chromed injected molded plastic, circa 1968.

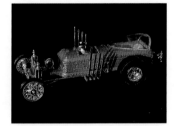

AMT: *Drag-u-la* hot rod, 1/25 scale, gold, colored injected molded plastic and chromed injected molded plastic, circa 1968.

Left
AMT: Ford 1932 hot rod roadster, red, 1/25 scale, custom assembled using parts from 12 different kits in diorama, colored injected molded plastic and chromed injected molded plastic, circa 1960.

Right
AMT: 1932 Ford Victoria, white, 1/25 scale, custom assembled as a drag car, colored injected molded plastic and chromed injected molded plastic, circa 1966.

Revell: *Outlaw*, Ed Roth hot rod-assembled kit, white and green, 1/25 scale, injected molded plastic and chromed injected molded plastic, later offered as *Canned Heat*, circa 1970.

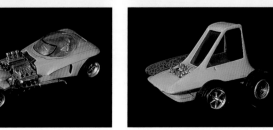

Revell: *Beatnik Bandit*, Ed Roth hot rod-assembled kit, white and bronze, 1/25 scale, injected molded plastic and chromed injected molded plastic, circa 1967.

Revell: *Mysterion*, Ed Roth hot rod-assembled kit, yellow, 1/25 scale, injected molded plastic and chromed injected molded plastic, circa 1965.

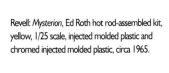

Revell: *Surfite*, Ed Roth hot rod surf buggy-assembled kit, yellow, 1/25 scale, injected molded plastic and chromed injected molded plastic, circa 1966.

Revell: Custom car parts kit, 1957 Chevrolet 283 V-8 engine kit, 1/25 scale, chromed injected plastic, circa 1968.

Revell: ZuZu, kit based on one of Ed Roth's hot rod monster kits, colored injected molded plastic and chromed injected molded plastic, circa 1983.

Monogram: Forty Niner series, the roadster 1932 Ford deuce *Little Red Rocket*, 5 inch, injected molded plastic, circa 1962.

Revell: *Outlaw*, Ed Roth hot rod-assembled kit, white and green, 1/25 scale, injected molded plastic and chromed injected molded plastic, re-popped kit, circa 1993.

MPC: *More American Graffiti*, 1932 Ford hot rod coupe. From the movie of the same name, yellow injected molded plastic and chromed injected molded plastic, circa 1979.

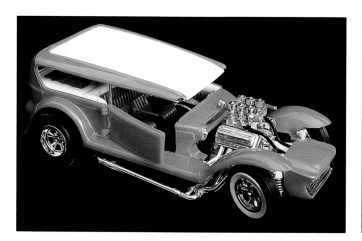

Monogram: *Li'l Coffin*, radical 1932 Ford showcar by Larry Farber, red and white, 1/24 scale custom assembled, colored injected molded plastic and chromed injected molded plastic, circa 1964.

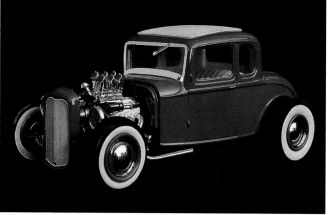

AMT: 1932 Ford coupe, purple, 1/25 scale, custom assembled as a street rod, colored injected molded plastic and chromed injected molded plastic, circa 1960.

When Mattel Inc. introduced their now-famous Hot Wheels toy cars in 1968, little did they know that these tiny wheeled-wonders would become an international favorite with kids and adults, strong enough to rival Barbie.

The variety of Hot Wheels is enormous today and the interest in collecting them is growing steadily. Collectors of these special-interest toys search for the early versions first. However, Mattel has recently re-issued some of the early Hot Wheels. This has not devalued the original editions, but rather made the models far more accessible to collectors than before.

Harry Bradley, the automotive and industrial designer, masterminded the Hot Wheels line for Mattel along with designing their flamed Hot Wheels logo. According to Harry, the Hot Wheels name was a direct derivation of the words "hot rod." Although the hot rods were loosely based on 1/64 scale this measure was quickly dropped and the cars were made approximately 2 1/2 inches long.

Bradley based his first Hot Wheels on his own custom El Camino, which the Alexander Brothers, in Detroit,

had customized for him. He quickly followed it with Ed Roth's *Beatnik Bandit*, the *Hot Heap*, the '27 T, the *Cheater*, and four other customs.

At first, all the Hot Wheels were made in either Hong Kong or Mexico. Within a year, Mattel sold so many Hot Wheels that the figure amounted to 1.7 cars per child in America, making it the largest selling toy in

Top Right

Neet Streeter, 1936 Ford coupe, blue, made in a variety of versions from 1969 on. First produced in Hong Kong, 1975. Many versions were made over the years. Yellow Ford 40s woodie wagon, first issued in 1980. Made in Malaysia in styles including Redline and Real Rider wheels.

Top Far Right

The *T-4-2* is a fantasy hot rod issued in 1971. On the right is the *Ice T* issued in 1972 and 1978.

Hot Heap, on the left, along with the *Cheetah* in the center, and Ed Roth s *Beatnik Bandit* on the right, were some of the first eight Hot Wheels issued in 1968. Designed by Harry Bradley, they were initially available in two colors. The *Cheetah* was based on *Car Craft s Dream Rod*, built by Bill Cushenbery; it was later re-issued as the *Python*.

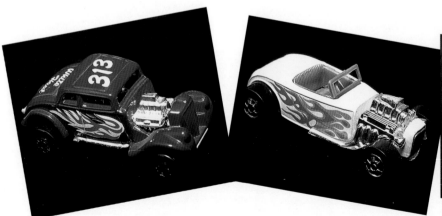

1934 Ford, three-window coupe, 1980.

White Heat, a 1934 Ford hot rod coupe, was the first of many variations of this body including a ZZ Top *Eliminator* version.

Street Rodder, 1932 Ford roadster hot rod, 1976. A real blown roadster that was chopped and channeled. Sold in a variety of colors including black and white.

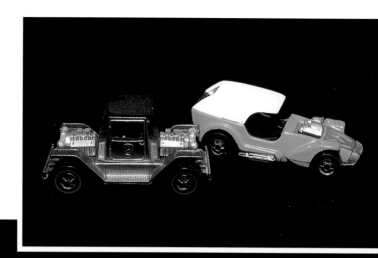

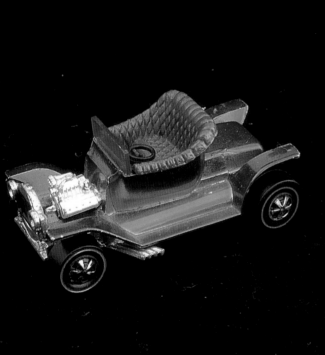

Left

Stagefright, made in Hong Kong. This is a replica of a famous showcar, 1977.

Right

Express Trucking, Ford C-cab, rear-engined hot rod truck, circa 1973.

the history of the toy industry. Over the years, Mattel has produced Hot Wheels in other countries, including India, Singapore, and Malaysia.

The variety of Hot Wheels models that Mattel has designed and produced is enormous. One collector claims to have in excess of 50,000 pieces! Obviously, only a small percentage of these are hot rods, but some of Mattel's most popular Hot Wheels have been hot rods and customs.

The name of the game with Hot Wheels is variation on a theme. The most basic variation which runs throughout Hot Wheels collecting is the wheels. Early versions featured the famous Redline wheels. They combined a five-spoke alloy wheel with a tire made of hard plastic highlighted by a fine redline ring. The tires featured a tapered tread surface which allowed the car to run on a fine band of plastic on the inner edge of the wheel. This narrow edge gave the cars an extremely low rolling resistance.

It is this wheel design in combination with the stainless steel axles that gave the little cars amazing speed when pushed across a hard floor or run on one of Hot Wheels' plastic tracks. They were so popular that the idea was copied by other companies.

One of the most popular of the competitive manufacturers is Johnny Lightning. Over the years, Johnny Lightning toys have had a few hot rod specific models which have recently been re-released along with a new set on popular funny cars. These Johnny Lightning toys are well worth collecting as they are well detailed and hot rod specific. Dozens of dime store toymakers from Asia have copied this idea over the years and there have been dozens of other similarly scaled hot rod toys.

The popularity of Hot Wheels "mini-car" toys came about not only because of their detail and speed but the fact that a kid could put them in a pocket and carry them around.

An early version, like the 1936 Ford coupe complete with scoop sticking through the hood, has appeared in a wide variety of color combinations, decals, wheels, and body detail over the past 30 years.

In late 1967, almost a year after Hot Wheels' beginning, a fully fendered T-roadster was introduced. This was the *Hot Heap*. It remained in the Hot Wheels line-up for many years and appeared in a wide variety of colors and interior combinations.

In 1970, Mattel also added to the market a classic-series 1931 Ford woody, a 1932 Ford vicky, and a 1936 coupe hot rod. The '36 coupe featured a trunk lid that flipped back to reveal a rumble seat and the body was scaled with a chopped roof.

The success of these spurred Mattel to create scaled replicas of a number of 1960's show rods in 1970. There was the *Demon,* which looked like *Li'l Coffin,* the *Red Baron* T-bucket, and Tom Daniel's *Paddy Wagon* show delivery. A few other hot rodded cars which weren't traditional hot rods were introduced in the early 1970s: *Classic Cord, Sir Rodney Roadster, T-4-2, Cockney Cab,* and several *Grass Hopper* Jeeps.

In 1976 the *Neet Streeter* '36 Ford coupe reappeared along with the first fenderless '32 highboy roadster called *Street Rodder.* This black-bodied, flamed roadster featured a blown engine with swoopy headers reaching back to the middle of the door. It has since been re-issued several times with Real Rider tires and in different colors.

A 1929 Ford sedan delivery called the *A-OK* appeared the next year. It is now considered highly collectible as it was only issued for a short time. It appeared in several variations of color with the rarest issue rolling on Goodyear-walled Real Rider tires.

There was a growing popularity of hot rodding and it was fortunate that Mattel's new head designer Larry Wood, who took over the project in around 1970, was a keen hot rodder. Larry reworked all existing hot rods and created a greater variety with new models during the 1970s by using new colors, accessories, and some restyling.

Two new hot rods appeared in 1980, the 1934 three-window and the 1940 woody. Since then many versions of them have appeared in different colors, but they are still basically the same version of the original issue. The '34 has appeared as a replica of the ZZ Top *Eliminator* coupe and as a two-tone version in a variety of colors and graphics. Today the black '34 with Real Rider tires is highly prized.

In 1983, Mattel issued the *Forties Ford 2-Door* in a wide variety of colors and updated it in 1984 as the *Fat Fendered '40.* In 1989, a chopped Hot Wheels called the *'32 Ford Delivery* and a 1927 T roadster called the *T-Bucket,* arrived. These new Hot Wheels hot rods are still on issue and have been offered in a huge variety of colors to please collectors. Mattel is also creating limited-issue collectors' editions for hot rod related activities such as rod runs and shows, which makes the collecting of Hot Wheels hot rods even more interesting.

Pricing is wildly wonderful. Collectors who know the hobby claim there are two prices for collectible Hot Wheels. California has one and the rest of the country has another. New Hot Wheels sell for 79¢ to 99¢ and the recent re-issues sell for $1.99 at local toy shops and drug stores. Used and abused examples of the early issues sell for $1 to $40. A perfect, in-the-pack first issue could sell for $250 or more. For detailed and accurate pricing refer to a Hot Wheels collectors' pricing guide.

The '32 vicky on the left was issued in 1969, along with the '36 Ford coupe in the center. They were both finished in spectra flame metallic paint. On the right is the *Sir Rodney Roadster* issued in 1974, based on a Lotus Super Seven.

1940s Ford two-door sedan flamed with Real Riders tires, made in Malaysia, 1982.

Silhouette, replica of Cushenbery Custom Car, 1967.

Dump truck, C-cab, Ford hot rod, made in Hong Kong, 1977.

Johnny Lightning, 1932 highboy roadster, one of many hot rods produced in the Johnny Lightning series.

On the left is the Johnny Lightning *TNT* hot rod with wildly raked bodywork, and on the right is the *Red Baron* show rod, first issued in 1969 and then re-issued as a 25th anniversary model.

Mutt Mobile, fantasy twin-engined hot rod, circa 1978.

Hot rodding's wild image was taken seriously by musicians in the 1950s, including Charlie Ryan, Johnny Bond, Jan and Dean, and the Beach Boys, who all used hot rodding as the icon of American youth at play.

Bill Haley didn't sing about hot rods but the cover of his *Shake Rattle and Roll* album, released on the Decca label in the late 1950s, shows the band in a cartooned hot rod roadster. Rock and roll music was as anti-social as hot rodding when it first emerged so "rock and rods" was a natural combination.

Country singers sang of their love for cars well before hot rodding rock and rollers put tracks on vinyl. The roots of hot rod music are in the 1940s with tunes including "Cadillac Boogie" by Jimmy Liggins, "Rocket 88" by Jackie Brenston, and "Hot Rod" by the Illinois Jacquet Orchestra. All were part of hot rod music's beginnings.

Around the beginning of the 1950s, Arkie Shibley and the Mountain Dew Boys sang "Hot Rod Race" on a gilt-edge 78 rpm record (#5021), and when Charlie Ryan and the Timberline Riders did "Hot Rod Lincoln" in 1955, its lyrics sang of the "kid in the Model A" referring to the lyrics in "Hot Rod Race," making a connection between the two songs. Both "Hot Rod Lincoln" and "Transfusion" by Nervous Norvus in 1958 further pressed the image of a hot rodder as an outlaw.

In the 1960s, hot rod music was created and sung by the Beach Boys, Dick Dale, the Rip Cords, the Vettes, the Astronauts, the Quads, and the Tokens, while Jan and Dean, the Surfaris, Hal Blaine, the Ventures, and The Darts also promoted tunes that embellished the hot rod image. They sang of fast cars, pretty girls, and cruising.

Interestingly, both Jan and Dean and the Beach Boys sang versions of the same songs including "Little Deuce Coupe" and "Drag City." Hot rodding and rock and roll were both youth-driven dreams and what better way to attract attention than to use hot rods to promote rock and roll music.

It is not well known that many of these hot rod albums were created using ghost bands. Gary Usher and Del-Fi record company owner, Bob Keane, used

Right
The Darts, Rod and the Cobras, and Jerry Cole pumped out hot rod music along with Sounds of Bonneville.

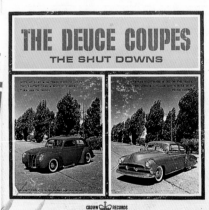

Charlie Ryan continued to feature hot rod music on his *Hot Rod* album with the tracks "Hot Rod Lincoln," "Hot Rod Race," and "Hot Rod Hades."

The Darts' *Hollywood Drag* album was on Bob Keane's Del-Fi label. *Hollywood Drag* featured the Darts playing tunes such as "Hollywood Drag," "Eliminator," and "Cruisin'."

The Shut Downs and the Deuce Coupes were a couple of Southern California sessions bands. Their album was a simple studio creation, like much of the surf music at the time. Presented on Crown Records, the album featured Dave Cunningham's 1940 Ford and Frank Livingston's gold and bronze 1949 custom Chevrolet.

Hot Rod Lincoln by Charlie Ryan offered "The new music and sounds of the Hot Rod set" with this album issued around 1958.

Bill Haley and his Comets issued Shake Rattle and Roll circa 1957. It featured a generic hot rod with the band cartooned riding along, while slicked-back Haley waved to the reader. It featured such great rock and roll songs as "Shake Rattle and Roll" and "Rock Around the Clock."

Hit City 64 from the Surfaris melded surf music with hot rod music. The Surfaris were an Orange County, California, group whose hits included "Wipe Out" and "Surfer Joe." On this album they offer a mix of hot rod and surf tunes including "Scatter Shield" and "Wax, Board and Woodie." Released on Decca in 1964, the album cover featured a Chevy-powered T-tub and a Ford Woodie.

studio musicians to play the hot rod tunes. It was not uncommon for record producers to invent a name for a band one month and then rename it the next month. Although some of these "bands" did not tour or perform outside the studio, the Deuce Coupes, The De-Fenders, and the Darts all recorded with Del-Fi using a sessions band known as the Wrecking Crew.

The Wrecking Crew musicians included Hal Blaine, Ray Pohlman, Carol Kaye, Lyle Ritz, Glen Campbell, Leon Russell, Larry Knechtel, Howard Roberts, and Michael Melvoin. Some of these performers went on to far greater heights with their own careers.

The most famous hot rod tune of all, apart from "Hot Rod Lincoln," must be "Little Deuce Coupe" by the Beach Boys on the Capital Records release of the album by the same name. The cover features a photo taken by Hot Rod magazine photographer, Eric Rickman, of Clarence "Chilli" Catallo's coupe, built by the Alexander Brothers in Detroit, and chopped and painted in the Barris shop in Los Angeles, California.

Since its release in the early 1960s, this album has sold millions of copies around the world; at least half a dozen of its songs were spun off as singles. Little Deuce Coupe was released as an eight-track, followed by cassette tape, and then as a compact disc, which must make it one of the all-time longest and best-selling collections of hot rod music in the industry. This album created more interest in hot rodding and drag racing than any other single piece of music. It carried ten hot rod songs, most of which have become associated with hot rodding and 1960s' California rock music.

Much of the music from this album was also released on later Beach Boys albums and compilations.

Other groups and singers, including the Shut Downs, the Kustom Kings, Johnny Bond, and the Deuce Coupes mixed in live sounds with music and ballads that were a cross mix of country and folk songs.

The Kustom Kings, with the help of George Barris, produced an album called Kustom City U.S.A. which featured photos of Barris-built custom and movie cars. These songs were sung and harmonized in a similar way to the Beach Boys ballads. They focused directly into the soul of the listener's interest in hot rods and fast cars, and although they were simple songs, they have entrenched themselves into three generations of music lovers.

Comedy albums were released, such as Hot Rod Hootenanny by the Weirdos, featuring such interesting tunes as "Chopped Nash," "Chrome It," and "Termites in my Woody."

Another interesting form of albums were hot rod recordings that incorporated the sounds of race cars, hot rods, and land speed cars from tracks and events. Albums like The Incredible Sights and Sounds of the Winternationals 1964 Pomona Championship Drag Races, produced by Audio Fidelity, featured the sounds of dragsters blasting down the track at the NHRA-sponsored Winternationals in Pomona, California.

Folks not usually associated with the record business became interested. The Hurst Corporation produced an album on the Indy NHRA Nationals and hot rod journalist Griffith Borgeson did a sound album from Bonneville Speed Week in 1960 which featured Mickey Thompson's ill-fated 409-miles per hour one-way record run in his land speed streamliner Challenger I.

Collecting these albums was once an easy task but with the passage of time they have become hard to find. Often the covers are damaged from use and records are scratched, but all is not lost for those who want the music. In the past couple of years there have been several re-issues of old material by Del-Fi and other recording studios. New Del-Fi re-releases include 32 Hot Rod Hits, with tracks by the Deuce Coupes, the Darts, and the De-Fenders. Satan Records has popped out Get a Board with music by the Torquettes, the Stings Rays, and Arlen Sanders. The all-time best compilation recording of hot rod music is Hot Rod Gang from Buffalo Bop; this is a great album, with tracks including such memorable tunes as "Spinner Hub Caps" by Pat Davis, "Full Racing Cam" by Eddie Ringo, and "Robin Hood and his '56 Ford" by Woody Ball.

Pricing is dependent upon rarity, the condition of the cover, and the condition of the record. Prices start at $3 and run to $200. New compact discs are $12.95 through $19.95.

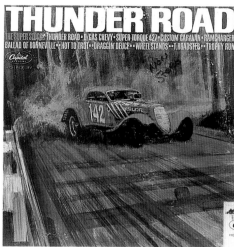

The Super Stocks' album *Thunder Road* was a great album of hot rod music including such interesting titles as "Super Torque 427," "D/Gas Chevy," "T.Roadster," and "The Ballad of Bonneville." Released on Capital Records.

Kustom City U.S.A., an album George Barris helped to create, was performed by a studio band called the Kustom Kings. The album cover featured Barris-built or modified cars, including the Oakland Roadster Show-winning *Emperor* roadster and the *El Capitola*, custom built by Sam Barris.

Hot Rod Rally was a studio album bannered with the *Hot Rod* magazine logo. Its flamed artwork and numerous little single Mooneyes created an interesting cover. The album has titles including "Night Rod," "Hot Rod City," and "Woody Walk." Released on Capital Records.

During the raging 1960s, crazy kinds of music were tried out. *Hot Rod Hootenanny* by the Weirdos was weird indeed. This was a cheap way for record producers to create an album without the expense of using a known band. Released on Capital, *Hot Rod Hootenanny* featured songs with such interesting titles as "Chopped Nash," "Hot Rod Hootenanny," "Termites in My Woody," and "Mr. Gasser."

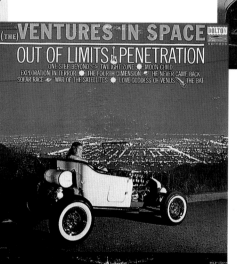

Hal Blaine named himself "The Drummer Man" and released this album called *Deuces, "T's," Roadsters & Drums*, on RCA Victor around 1965. The cover featured Hal at his drums on the beachfront in California surrounded by four hot rod roadsters. Tracks from this album have nifty titles like "Pop the Chute," "Gear Stripper," and "Nashville Coupé."

The Ventures' album *(The) Ventures in Space* featured a cute T-bucket roadster overlooking the lights of Los Angeles. Released on Dolton Records, this instrumental album offered tracks with titles that had little relationship to the musical content, circa 1964.

Left

Jerry Kole and the Strokers delivered *Hot Rod Alley* to the market around 1963. The cover featured George Barris's *Ala Kart* roadster pickup which had won at the Oakland Roadster Show in 1958 and 1959. The music on the album included "My Little Hot Rod," "Pealin Out," and "409 Woodie." *Hot Rod Alley* was released on Crown Records.

Right

Competition Coupe was a strange title for a record featuring a pair of roadsters on the cover, and yes, that is the flamed roadster owned and built by Tom McMullen on the right. The Astronauts, who were originally from Boulder, Colorado, created their own mix of surf and hot rod music after signing with RCA Victor in 1963. They toured like the Surfaris and had a couple of mild hits including a tune called "Baja," which was written by Lee Hazelwood, circa 1964.

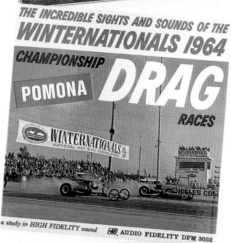

Left

Audio Fidelity released this live sounds album entitled, *The Incredible Sights and Sounds of the Winternationals 1964 Pomona Championship Drag Races*. It is possibly the longest title of any record. The cover featured a pair of fuelers leaving the line at the championships, and the record featured various kinds of race cars making passes at the meet.

Right

This live sound recording was backed by the Hurst Corporation, makers of Hurst Shifters and the NHRA. Recorded at the NHRA Nationals in Indianapolis, Indiana, it was better prepared than other earlier albums; it mixed interviews with drivers, race car sounds, and narration.

Left

The Rip Cords was a studio band that had some hits. They played under a variety of names, including the Rogues and Bruce and Terry. As the Rip Cords they did do some touring and their greatest hit was "Hey Little Cobra" released in November 1963. This track is still popular today with 1960s music radio stations. Their album, *Three Window Coupe*, mixed surf and hot rod music with tracks like "Surf City" and "Hot Rod U.S.A."

Right

This compilation album, featuring "TV" Tommy Ivo and his fuel dragster on the cover, mixed music from the Quads, the Grand Prix, and the Customs, on a Vault recording. The album was another of Gary Usher's studio-produced albums and could easily be confused with other studio hot rod albums produced at the time.

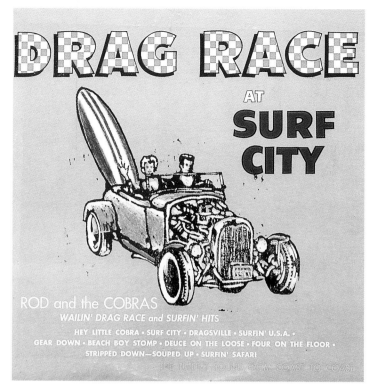

Rod and the Cobras was another studio band, and their album, *Drag Race at Surf City*, melded surf and hot rod music. The album covered the Rip Cords' "Hey Little Cobra" along with other tracks such as "Deuce on the Loose," "Stripped Down—Souped Up," and "Surfin' U.S.A." The album cover featured a neat illustration of a Deuce roadster toting a longboard, circa 1965.

Hot Rod Rumble was the soundtrack to the movie of the same name. It featured a Hilborn injected, Buick-powered T with Leigh Snowden and Richard Hartunian on the cover. Released on Liberty in Spectra Sonic Sound, circa 1958.

Top
The Deuce Coupes was one of Bob Keane's studio bands. His Del-Fi recording studios cranked out lots of surf and hot rod music, and on the album *Hot Rodders' Choice*, the Deuces Coupes recorded "Gear Masher," "Smooth Stick," and "Tijuana Gasser." Circa 1965.

Middle
This Beach Boys album *Little Deuce Coupe* is one of the all-time best-selling records in the music industry. It was released in the mid-1960s and has been made available in every form of music recording from single record, extended play, album, reel-to-reel, 8-track, cassette, and compact disc. It is the perfect hot rod music album—so many great tunes. Eric Rickman's great photo of Clarence Catallo's chopped and channeled '32 coupe graces the cover.

Bottom
Charlie Ryan's *Hot Rod Lincoln Drags Again!* album featured "The Authentic Sounds of Country & Western Music." This Hilltop recording tracked tunes such as "Hot Rod Guitar," "Hot Rod Race," and "Cadillac Bounce." The cover displays a neat old blown altered dragster with Ryan's guitar laying on the front frame rails.

35

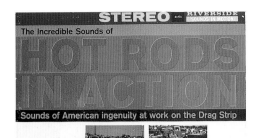

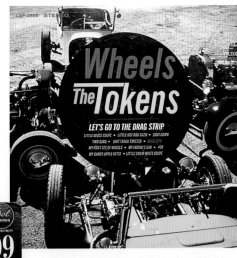

Hot Rods in Action was an off-brand, live sound recording of drag racing created in stereo in the mid-1960s. It was subtitled "Sounds of American ingenuity at work on the drag strip."

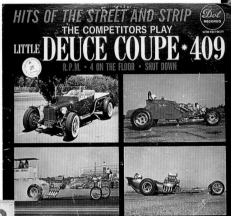

As a hot rod music album this Tokens album, *Wheels*, was another studio fabrication. The Tokens did have a great hit called "The Lion Sleeps Tonight." The Tokens' harmonizing mixed the essence of the sounds of Jan & Dean and the Beach Boys into tunes including "My First Set of Wheels," "My Candy Apple Vette," "Little "Deuce Coupe," and "Shut Down." Released on RCA Victor, circa 1965.

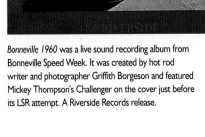

The Competitors were a studio band who recorded on Dot Records. Their *Hits of the Street and Strip* album featured "Little Deuce Coupe," "409," and "Cheater Slicks."

Bonneville 1960 was a live sound recording album from Bonneville Speed Week. It was created by hot rod writer and photographer Griffith Borgeson and featured Mickey Thompson's Challenger on the cover just before its LSR attempt. A Riverside Records release.

Wax 'Em Down! Vol. 1 is a compilation album currently offered which includes a mass of famous and not-so-famous hot rod and surf music. It features a photo of a couple of guys wearing Roth airbrushed monster sweatshirts. This photo previously appeared on the cover of *Sports Illustrated.*

The New Dimensions' album *Deuces and Eights* was another surf/hot rod instrumental album but it featured some cool bongo playing. Recorded and released on Sutton it was one of three records from the New Dimensions. "Black Top," "Deuces and Eights," "Totaled," and "Junker" give you an idea of the album's direction, circa 1965.

For paper collectors, hot rodding offers a bountiful mass of material. There are wonderful collections to be assembled in series with books, annuals, manuals, and pictorials.

Collecting nonfiction hot rod books has two separate arenas, hardback and softbound. Early collectors' hardback books on hot rodding are rare and may only amount to half a dozen titles. These were books from the conventional publishing trade which rarely dabbled in "counterculture" publishing. Today there is a solid offering of such material but most of it is still in print and is not included in this book.

One of the few items of note from the late 1940s was the softbound *Veda Orr's Hot Rod Pictorial* published by Floyd Clymer. This book was a pictorial of early lakes, speedway racing, and street rodding. It is in black and white with 48 pages, including photos and superb illustrations by Dick Teague, who later

went on to become head of American Motors' design studio.

Hardback collectors' editions from major publishing houses, including the 1959 edition of *The Complete Book of Hot Rodding* from Prentice-Hall are quite rare, especially in good condition. Surprisingly, it was authored by Robert E. Petersen and the staff at *Hot Rod* magazine, which makes Petersen one of the few sources of this early hot rod material. Another smaller hardback was *Hot Rods: How to Build & Race Them* by the former managing editor of *Hot Rod* magazine, John Christy, and it was brought out about the same time.

The other area for collectors is in softbound books from Petersen Publishing. It is these books that are the most exciting, offering condensed photo collections, race features, and technical and how-to article. This kind of book is referred to as a "one shot"

Fawcett Publications: *True's Automobile Yearbook*, No. 1, 128 pages, 8x11 1/2 inches in color and black & white, 1951, contains feature stories from all parts of the automobile world.

Bobbs-Merrill: *Hot Rods: How to Build & Race Them* by John Christy, 360 pages, 6x9 inches in black & white, circa 1960.

Prentice-Hall: *The Complete Book of Hot Rodding* by Robert E. Petersen, 224 pages, 8x11 inches in black & white, 1959, a dull book but still worth having.

Floyd Clymer: *Veda Orr's Hot Rod Pictorial*, 48 pages, 11x8 1/2 inches in black & white, 1949, features photos and stories from the speedways, dry lakes, and early street rodding, plus Dick Teague's dry lakes illustrations.

publication and was offered to hot rodders as something new to buy from the newsstand. They have become highly collectible today and are still relatively cheap and easy to find at most hot rod swap meets.

Back in the 1950s and early 1960s, Petersen Publishing was one of few hot rod publishers so there is little else to collect from this time. However, they published abundantly with an enormous and still ongoing offering of full-sized annuals, yearbooks, how-to books, and specialty issues.

The first one-shot book published by Petersen was the *Hot Rod Annual*. It was produced as a 128-page "little book" and sold for 75¢. (This is covered in the chapter on "Little Books.")

In 1961, Petersen changed the format and introduced the *Hot Rod Magazine Yearbook* for $2. The smaller *Hot Rod Annual* was not dropped at that time but remained in the "little book" format. Interestingly, the contents of the 1961 *Annual* focused on drag racing while the *Yearbook* was mostly hot rodding. Some later *Yearbooks* were also issued in hardback.

The early 1960s, *Yearbooks* spawned a massive outpouring of one-shot books that continues to this day. Petersen Publishing still issues upwards of 15 new automotive one-shot books each year. Over the years titles have included *Rod & Custom Annual, Custom Car Yearbook, Complete Buyers Guide to Kit Cars, Body and*

Paint, Classic Trucks, The Complete Chevrolet Book, The Complete Ford Book, and multiple editions and re-issues of *The Best of Hot Rod*.

The Best of Hot Rod has been an enormously successful title and has been re-issued with varied contents several times. The first issue of *The Best of Hot Rod* was a thick 192-page softbound book which contained a large section of the best photos from *Hot Rod* magazine during the previous 30 years. The photos are heavily captioned and it is a prize to have in any library. The cover has a shot of a black '32 roadster in a garage with a girl chewing gum while guys work on the roadster. This issue is a must for any collection.

The rarest and most interesting two issues of *Custom Car Yearbook* were published in 1963 and 1964. These 224-page softbound books from Petersen Publishing are teeming with nostalgic imagery and technical information. They are a must for custom collectors, but they're hard to find.

Many of the books are previously used magazine material, repackaged into a thicker, better bound edition. Unlike the magazines from which these stories were pulled, the one-shots did not contain any advertising which is a distinct plus as they are filled from cover to cover with stories and photo features. The selling price was $2 for many years until *The Best of Hot Rod* came out, then it jumped to $9.95—very expensive at the time.

Some articles in these editions were better presented than the original magazine stories with fresh layouts and new photos. One of the best in this series is the 1972 edition of *The Complete Ford Book*. With 192 pages it is a great source covering Ford's performance history from early hot rodding to Indy, Bonneville, Le Mans, and NHRA drag racing, a must for Ford literature fans with excellent technical articles and a 7-page "Major Engine Specs" chart for 1954 to 1972 Fords.

Pricing for hardbacks varies widely. Book collectors are asking $25 to $40 for these issues while swap meet prices range from $10 to $25. Softbound Petersen *Annuals* run the same kind of pricing differential, starting in swap meets at $5 and going as high as $25. *Yearbooks,* especially the early ones, run $10 to $30, with the *Custom Yearbooks* trading hands as high as $40. East Coast prices are generally lower than the above West Coast prices.

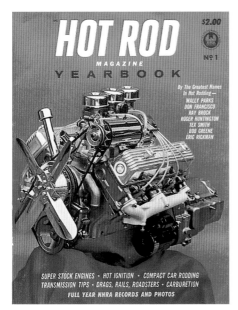

Petersen Publishing: *Hot Rod Magazine Yearbook*, No. 1, 224 pages, 8x11 inches in black & white, 1961, technical and feature stories assembled from *Hot Rod* magazine. A must for any collection.

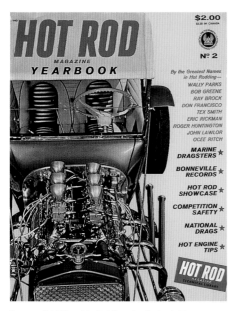

Petersen Publishing: *Hot Rod Magazine Yearbook*, No. 2, 224 pages, 8x11 inches in black & white, 1962, technical and feature stories assembled from *Hot Rod* magazine. A must for any collection.

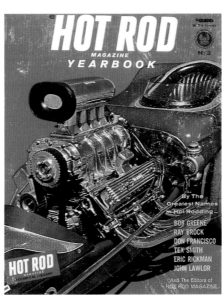

Petersen Publishing: *Hot Rod Magazine Yearbook*, No. 3, 224 pages, 8x11 inches in black & white, 1963, technical and feature stories assembled from *Hot Rod* magazine. A must for any collection.

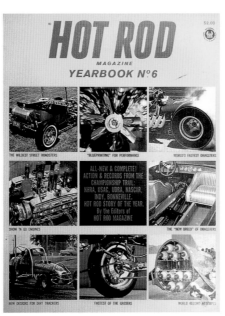

Petersen Publishing: *Hot Rod Magazine Yearbook*, No. 6, 224 pages, 8x11 inches in black & white, 1966, is a must for any collection with a broad spread of stories technical, and features, assembled from *Hot Rod* magazine.

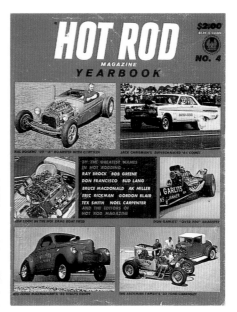

Petersen Publishing: *Hot Rod Magazine Yearbook*, No. 4, 224 pages, 8x11 inches in black & white, 1964, technical and feature stories assembled from *Hot Rod* magazine. There's a lot of drag racing, but it's still a must.

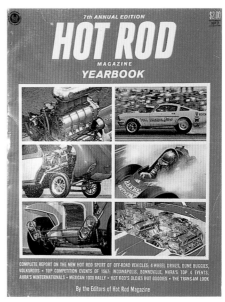

Petersen Publishing: *Hot Rod Magazine Yearbook*, No. 7, 224 pages, 8x11 inches in black & white, 1967, technical and feature stories with an emphasis on drag racing. It includes four-wheel and dune buggy stories from *Hot Rod* magazine. A must for any collection.

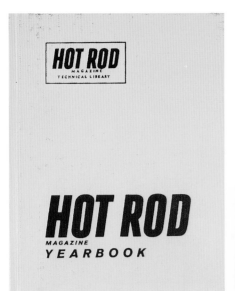

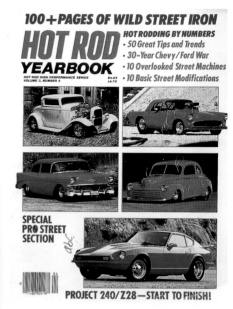

Petersen Publishing: Hot Rod Magazine Yearbook, No. 8, 192 pages, 11x8 inches, yellow cover, hardback edition with black & white, 1968, technical and feature stories assembled from *Hot Rod* magazine. There are a lot of Baja, Bonneville and Volkswagen stories. It is a must for any collection.

Petersen Publishing: *Hot Rod Magazine Yearbook*, Vol. 3, No. 4, 174 pages, 8x11 inches in black & white, and color, 1985, technical and feature stories assembled from *Hot Rod* magazine a must for any collection.

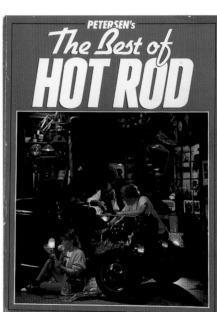

Petersen Publishing: *The Best of Hot Rod*, 190 pages, 8x11 inches black & white and color, 1981, feature stories assembled from *Hot Rod* magazine. A must for any collection.

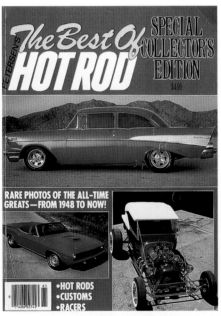

Petersen Publishing: *The Best of Hot Rod*, Special Collectors' Edition, 176 pages, 8x11 inches in black & white and color, 1986, photo features assembled from 40 years of *Hot Rod* magazine. A must for any collection.

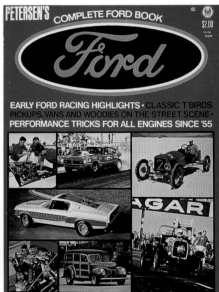

Petersen Publishing: *The Complete Ford Book*, 192 pages, 8x11 inches assembled in black & white 1972 technical and photo features about Fords from the pages of *Hot Rod* magazine. An absolute must for any Ford fan.

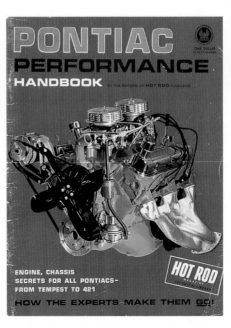

Petersen Publishing: *Pontiac Performance Handbook*, 96 pages, 8x11 inches assembled in black & white, 1963, technical and photo features about Pontiacs in *Hot Rod* magazine.

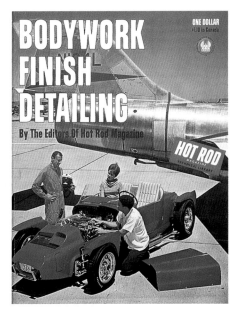

Petersen Publishing: *Bodywork Finish Detailing*, 96 pages, 8x11 inches assembled in black & white, 1964, technical and photo features about hot rod fabrication in steel and aluminum.

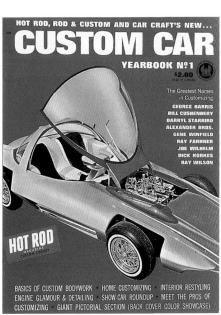

Petersen Publishing: *Custom Car Yearbook*, No. 1, 224 pages, 8x11 inches assembled in black & white 1963 technical and photo features about custom cars and their construction. This issue features Bill Cushenbery's *Silhouette* on the cover. An absolute must for any custom car fan.

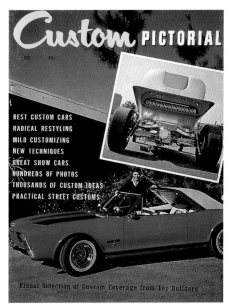

Argus Publishers: *Custom Pictorial* #206, 82 pages, 8x11 inches, black & white photos, 1965, stories on custom cars and hot rods featuring George Barris's *Villa Riviera* with James Darren. This one is rare.

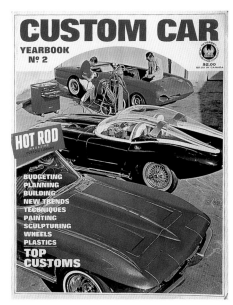

Petersen Publishing: *Custom Car Yearbook*, No. 2, 224 pages, 8x11 inches assembled in black & white, 1964, technical and photo features about custom cars and their construction. This second issue is also an absolute must for any custom car fan. The cover features a scene at the Barris shop with the *Manta Ray* 'Vette, a custom XKE, and a custom Falcon under construction.

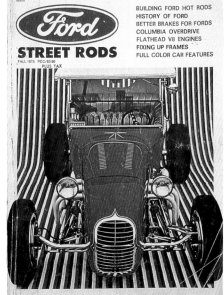

Challenge Publications: *Ford Street Rods*, 178 pages, 8x11 inches assembled in black & white, 1975, technical and photo features about Ford custom cars and hot rods from *Rod Action* magazine.

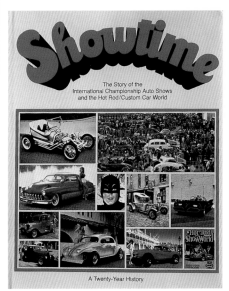

Promotional Displays Incorporated: *Showtime* by Bob Larivee, Sr., 231 pages, 9x11 inches in color and black & white, 1980. This is a hardback condensed history of the International Championship Auto Shows.

Hot rodders who grew up in the 1950s received their first introduction to hot rodding from reading rodding magazines and what was known as "the little books." Two forms of these little books existed. The first form was the early magazines, including *Honk, Hop Up, Car Craft,* and *Rod and Custom.* The second was the small-format hot rodders' reference books, which are still known as "little books."

For many years hot rodders referred to what they had seen or read as, "I saw it in one of the little books." These were the hot rodders' reference guides and came from a wide variety of sources and publishers. In the magazine trade, books like these were considered one-shots as they were published only once without regard to creating reprints or even further issues in a series.

In California, Petersen Publishing branched out to produce these little books in 1951 and the first publication was created by the editors at *Motor Trend* magazine. It was titled *Custom Cars #101* and

sold through their new Trends Inc. division. This book, with a bright yellow cover, depicted a green sports roadster and a classic custom 1947 Ford and is considered the number one collectors' item. It is filled with great photos from 1948 to 1950 of hot rods and customs.

Petersen went on to create several series using the 128-page formula for little books including their first *Hot Rod Annuals.* A *Custom Cars Annual* was added, and the idea was further expanded with little books that focused on drag racing, karting, sports cars, and how-to books. By the beginning of 1962 over a hundred editions had been published.

However the trend was not only a West Coast concept. Fawcett Publications in Greenwich, Connecticut, started an ongoing series of little books enti-

Right
George Barris created a mass of technical books filled with how-to details and styling ideas. These books were very popular in their day.

California Bill's Hot Rod Manual by Fred W. Fisher, 124 pages, 5 1/4x8 1/4 inches, black & white, 1949, softback technical manual on building hot rod roadsters and engines. It's the classic early how-to hot rod book, recently republished in 1996 by the author.

California Bill's Chevrolet Speed Manual by Fred W. Fisher, 124 pages, 5 1/4x8 1/4 inches, black & white, 1951, softback technical manual on building hot rod Chevrolet engines. It's another classic early how-to hot rod book.

Left: Fawcett Publications: *Best Hot Rods* by Jaderquist and Borgeson, 96 pages, 9 1/4x6 1/2 inches, black & white, 1955, annual Bonneville story, NHRA, street rod, and hot rod racing stories, 1953. Right: Fawcett Publications: *How to Build and Race Hot Rods* by Griffith Borgeson, 96 pages, 9 1/4 x 6 1/2 inches, black & white, annual Bonneville story, NHRA, street rod, and hot rod racing stories.

CUSTOMIZING WITH FIBERGLASS
BY GEORGE BARRIS
35c
40c IN CANADA
S-531

CUSTOM CAR ENGINES
BY GEORGE BARRIS
35c
40c IN CANADA
S-530

CUSTOM DASHBOARDS AND DETAILING
By George Barris
35c
40c IN CANADA
S-528

Custom UPHOLSTERING
By George Bar
25c
S-524

CUSTOM SCOOPS and Sculpturing

Customizing FINS and TAILLIGHTS
25c
S-515

CUSTOM CAR GRILLES
25c
S-506

TREND BOOK NO. 102
Hot Rods
75c
COMPLETE DATA ON OUT-STANDING STREET AND COMPETITION HOT RODS
160 PAGES!
72
BUILDING TIPS — ENGINE AND CHASSIS
By the Editors of Hot Rod Magazine

SPORT CARS and HOT RODS
75c BOOK 109
Alfa Romeo Sport Car
150 MPH Merlin's Hot Rod
FOREIGN AND U.S. SPORT CARS • HOW TO HOP UP YOUR CAR
TOM McCAHILL • KEN PURDY • JOHN BENTLEY

HOT ROD Handbook
75c BOOK 129
Hendrickson-Turner Class B Modified Coupe
80 D
THE HOTTEST RODS • HOW TO BUILD A HOT ROD TRIALS AND DRAGS • SPEED EQUIPMENT REVIEW
Howard Johansen's 170 mph Twin Tanker
HOP-UP HINTS • CLUBS AND ORGANIZATIONS

Petersen Publishing Trend Books: *Hot Rods*, No. 102, 160 pages, 9 1/4x6 1/2 inches, black and white, circa 1953, with cool color cover featuring roadster, a coupe, and a dry lakes tank. This is the second little book from Petersen and is must for any collection

Fawcett Publications: *Sports Cars and Hot Rods* by McCahill, Purdy and Bentley, 96 pages, 9 1/4x6 1/2 inches, black & white, 1953. Early sports car, street rod, and hot rod racing stories.

Fawcett Publications: *Hot Rod Handbook*, 144 pages, 9 1/4x6 1/2 inches, black & white, 1953. Early street rod and hot rod racing stories with features on Bonneville cars and events.

43

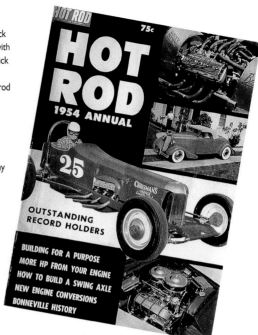

Popular Mechanics: *Hot Rod Handbook and Directory of America's Finest Speed Shops*, by George Hill, 144 pages, 9 1/4x6 1/2 inches, black & white, 1954. One of the classic little books with great cover art featuring what appears to be Dick Flint's '29 roadster. Excellent coverage of Bonneville in 1953 with some how-to and hot rod organization stories. A must have.

Petersen Publishing: *Hot Rod 1954 Annual*, 96 pages, 9 1/4x6 1/2 inches, black & white with color cover featuring the Chrisman roadster, 1954. Technical stories on hot rodding and many kinds of street and race rods.

tled *Sports Cars and Hot Rods* around 1950 with the help of editors and writers like Griffith Borgeson, Wayne Thoms, and Louis Hochman.

The most highly prized of these are the editions by Griffith Borgeson as they featured great photos of the best hot rods, Bonneville and drag racing stories, and have become an excellent source for researchers and bench-racing truth seekers. Most of these issues ran to 144 pages and were lavishly illustrated with titles including *Best Hot Rods, Hot Rod Handbook, How-To Book of Hot Rods, Griffith Borgeson on Hot Rods,* and *How to Build High Performance Hot Rods*. *Mechanix Illustrated*, a Fawcett magazine title, also offered a series of little books.

Other publishing houses got on the same wagon. Popular Mechanics Company in Chicago, Illinois, created another of the classic little books in 1954 entitled *Popular Mechanics Hot Rod Handbook*. Written by George Hill, Bonneville record holder and charter member of the 200 MPH Club, it featured a color illustration of three hot rodders working on what appears to be Dick Flint's 1929 roadster. Flint's roadster had appeared on the cover of *Hot Rod* magazine in May 1952 complete with bright red body work. On the cover of *Hot Rod Handbook*, the roadster's color had changed to pale green.

The Popular Mechanics Company's issue of *Hot Rod Handbook* from 1954 rates as one of the most highly prized of little books. It should not be confused with the similarly titled *Hot Rod Handbook* that Fawcett issued in 1958.

In 1949 California, Bill Fisher created the *California Bill's Hot Rod Manual* as a hands-on, how-to-build

hot rods book. It was illustrated with cutaway drawings, welding instructions, engineering ideas, and engine building techniques. It was also illustrated with excellent artwork by Tom Medley, writer, photographer, and cartoonist for *Hot Rod* magazine. California Bill also published the *Chevrolet Speed Manual*, the *A-V8 Manual,* and the *Four Barrel Manual*. Today, *California Bill's Hot Rod Manual* is considered a classic and has just been reproduced.

A new series of little books and one-shots emerged during the 1960s. Petersen Publishing created an ongoing series of books under the Spotlite Books imprint which were both pictorial and technical, and covered subjects ranging from model hot rods and customs to real chassis, engine, paint, and bodywork. The great camera work of George Barris and his eye for detail created some of the Spotlite's best issues on all parts of the hot rod and custom hobby. Some of the titles were *10 Top Hot Rods, Custom Painting Techniques, Custom Car Grilles,* and *Custom Pickups*.

Pricing of these issues is always wide open. Early Fawcett books sell for $25 to $40 from dealers, depending upon their condition, yet can still be found in swap meets for $5 to $10. Expect to pay top dollar for the early Trend Inc. *Custom Cars (#101)*. It's worth every cent. Also expect to pay a similar price for Popular Mechanics' *Hot Rod Handbook*. *Hot Rod* magazine annuals command prices ranging from $25 to $40 for 1950s' editions and $5 to $10 for 1960s'. The Petersen's Spotlite series of little books varies, at some swap meets you will find them for $5 a copy while at others they might run $15 to $20.

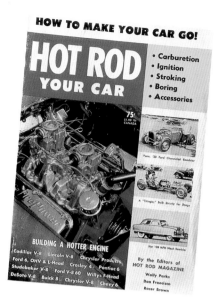

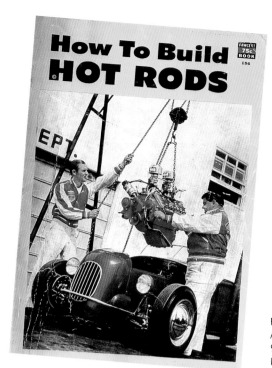

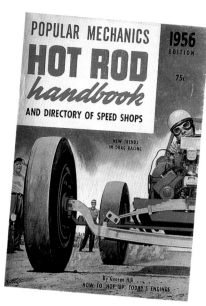

Petersen Publishing: *Hot Rod Your Car*, 96 pages, 9 1/4x6 1/2 inches, black & white with color cover, circa 1955. Technical stories on hot rodding and all kinds of street cars.

Fawcett Publications: *How To Build Hot Rods*, 144 pages, 9 1/4x6 1/2 inches, black & white, circa 1954. Early street rod and hot rod building stories.

Popular Mechanics: *Hot Rod Handbook and Directory of America's Finest Speed Shops*, by George Hill, 144 pages, 9 1/4x6 1/2 inches, black & white, 1956. Another classic little book with great cover art. A must have.

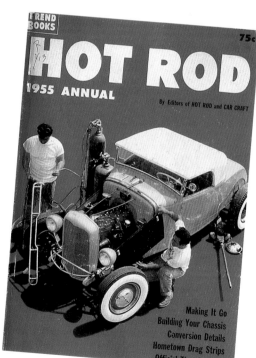

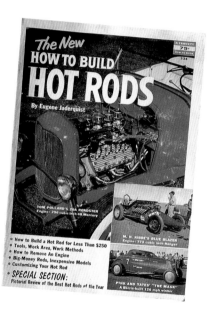

Petersen Publishing: *Hot Rod 1956 Annual*, 96 pages, 9 1/4x6 1/2 inches, black & white with cover featuring an engine swap; Ak Miller on the left, 1956. Technical stories on hot rodding and drag racing condensed from *Hot Rod* magazine.

Petersen Publishing: *Hot Rod 1955 Annual*, 96 pages, 9 1/4x6 1/2 inches, black & white, 1955. Striking red cover with a yellow highboy roadster. Technical stories on hot rodding and all kinds of street and race rods.

Fawcett Publications: *The New How To Build Hot Rods*, Eugene Jaderquist, 128 pages, 9 1/4x6 1/2 inches, black & white, circa 1956. Early street rod and hot rod building stories.

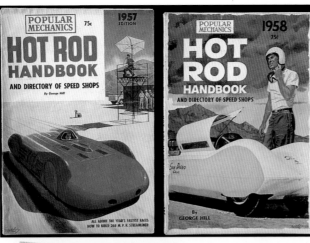
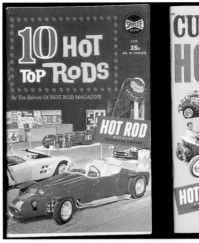
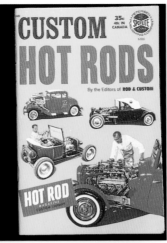

Top Left

Left: Popular Mechanics: *Hot Rod Handbook and Directory of America's Finest Speed Shops*, by George Hill, 144 pages, 9 1/4x6 1/2 inches, black & white, 1957. Another classic little book with great Bonneville cover art. A must have. Right: Popular Mechanics: *Hot Rod Handbook and Directory of America's Finest Speed Shops*, by George Hill, 144 pages, 9 1/4x6 1/2 inches, black & white, 1958. Another classic little book with great Bonneville cover art. A must have.

Top Right

Left: Petersen Publishing Spotlite Books: *10 Top Hot Rods*, by *Hot Rod* magazine editors, 64 pages, 8x5 inches, black & white with color cover, 1963. Photo stories on the best hot rods. Right: Petersen Publishing Spotlite Books: *Custom Hot Rods*, by *Rod and Custom* magazine editors, 64 pages, 8x5 inches, black & white with color cover, 1963. Photo and technical stories on hot rod building.

Left

Fawcett Publications: *Hot Rod Handbook*, by Louis Hochman, 144 pages, 9 1/4x6 1/2 inches, black & white, 1958. Covers street rods and drag racing with expert technical features.

Right

Fawcett Publications: *Griffith Borgeson on Hot Rods*, by Griffith Borgeson, 144 pages, 9 1/4x6 1/2 inches, black & white, 1959. Color cover features Roth's *Tweetie Pie* and Mickey Thompson's *Challenger*. Book covers street rods, Bonneville, and drag racing with expert technical features.

Left

Petersen Publishing: *Hot Rod 1958 Annual*, 96 pages, 9 1/4x6 1/2 inches, black & white with color cover featuring a flamed 1940 Ford, 1958. Technical stories on hot rodding, Bonneville and drag racing condensed from *Hot Rod* magazine.

Right

Petersen Publishing: *Hot Rod 1959 Annual*, 96 pages, 9 1/4x6 1/2 inches, black & white with color cover featuring Barris's *Ala Kart* and Romeo Palamides' dragster, 1959. Technical stories on hot rodding, Bonneville and drag racing condensed from *Hot Rod* magazine.

Above Right

Left: Petersen Publishing Spotlite Books: *20 Top Customs*, by George Barris, 64 pages, 8x5 inches, black & white with color cover, 1962. Photo features on the best customs. Right: Petersen Publishing Spotlite Books: *Custom Pickups*, by George Barris, 64 pages, 8x5 inches, black & white with color cover, 1963. Photo and technical stories on custom pickups.

Middle Right

Left: Petersen Publishing Spotlite Books: *Steering and Chassis*, by *Hot Rod* magazine editors, 48 pages, 8x5 inches, black & white with color cover, 1962. How-to photo stories. Right: Petersen Publishing Spotlite Books: *Bodywork*, by *Hot Rod* magazine editors, 64 pages, 8x5 inches, black & white with color cover, 1965. Photo and technical stories on fiberglass and metal body building.

Custom Handbook No. 1: *Trophy-Taking Custom Ideas*. Small book featuring the *Jade Idol* on the cover with photo details inside on custom building ideas and techniques, circa 1962.

J. Lowell Pratt-American Sports Library: *The Hot Rod Handbook*, by Fred Horsley, 212 pages, 7x4 inches, this issue 1965. Some photos and illustrations. Originally released in 1957 as *Hot Rod It—And Run For Fun*.

Petersen Publishing/Signet Books: *Super Tuning*, 416 pages, 7x4 inches, paperback, photos and illustrations re-hashed from *Hot Rod* magazine. One of a series of books released by Signet.

Left: Petersen Publishing Spotlite Books: *Customizing with Fiberglass*, by George Barris, 62 pages, 8x5 inches, black & white with color cover, 1963. How-to photo stories. Right: Petersen Publishing Spotlite Books: *Custom Car Grilles*, by George Barris, 64 pages, 8x5 inches, black & white with color cover, 1961. Photo and technical stories on building custom grilles.

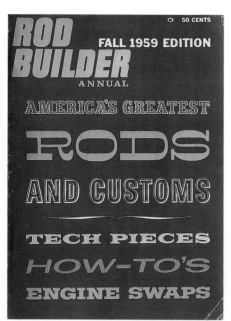

Rod Builder Annual 1959, 96 pages, 9 1/4x6 1/2 inches, black & white with color cover, 1959. Technical stories on building hot rods and customs, and photo features on rods and customs.

Post Publications: *Custom re-Styling*, by Dan Post, 192 pages, 9 1/4x6 1/2 inches, black & white, third edition, 1951. Many early customs in this revised edition. Great books if you can find them.

Fawcett Publications: *Best Hot Rods*, by Griffith Borgeson, 144 pages, 9 1/4x6 1/2 inches, black & white, 1960. Bonneville, street rod, drag racing, and go-kart stories with some technical features.

Petersen Publishing: *Hot Rod 1960 Annual*, 96 pages, 9 1/4x6 1/2 inches, black & white with color cover, 1960. Technical stories on hot rodding, Bonneville, and drag racing condensed from *Hot Rod* magazine.

Petersen Publishing: *Hot Rod 1961 Annual*, 96 pages, 9 1/4x6 1/2 inches, black & white with color cover, 1960. Technical stories on hot rodding and drag racing condensed from *Hot Rod* magazine.

Fawcett Publications: *The How-To Book of Hot Rods*, Wayne Thoms & Griffith Borgeson, 144 pages, 9 1/4x6 1/2 inches, black & white, 1961. Bonneville, street rod, and drag racing stories along with "Rodding in Russia," and "Welding Made Easy."

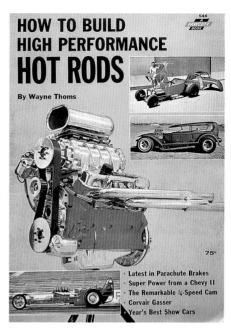

Popular Mechanics: *Hot Rod Annual*, by George Hill, 128 pages, 9 1/4x6 1/2 inches, black & white, 1961. The sixth little book from *Popular Mechanics* and another classic. Not as well printed as the 1950s editions but still great Bonneville coverage.

Fawcett Publications: *How to Build High Performance Hot Rods*, by Wayne Thoms, 110 pages, 9 1/4x6 1/2 inches, black & white, 1961. Cover features a GMC blown Dodge and *Li'l Coffin*. Book features customs, drag racing, and hot rods.

Fawcett Publications: *Hot Rod Handbook*, by Griffith Borgeson, 144 pages, 9 1/4x6 1/2 inches, black & white, circa 1959. Street rod, drag racing, and go-kart stories.

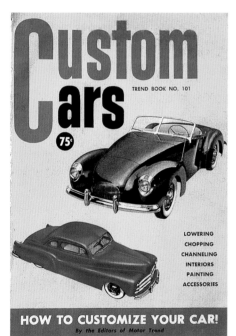

Petersen Publishing Trend Book: *Custom Cars*, No. 101, 126 pages, 9 1/2x6 1/2 inches, black and white with cool color cover featuring two customs, 1951. This is the first Petersen little book and is stuffed with the great early customs and includes some neat technical stories. Advertised on the back cover of *Motor Trend* in October 1951, 75¢. This is the classic little book and a must for any collection.

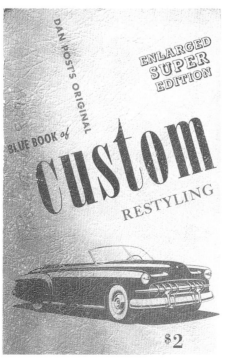

Petersen Publishing Trend Books: *Restyle Your Car*, by Jim Potter, 96 pages, 9 1/4x6 1/2 inches, black & white with color cover, circa 1958. Photo and technical stories on custom car building.

Post Publications: *Blue Book of Custom Restyling*, Dan Post, 192 pages, 9 1/4x6 1/2 inches, black & white, second edition, 1952. Tons of early customs in the entire book series. Four in the series with some repeat material used in all four books.

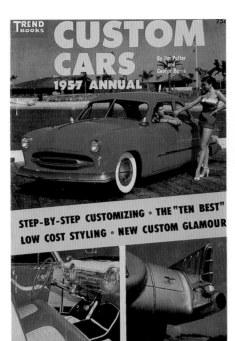

Petersen Publishing Trend Books: *Custom Cars 1957 Annual*, by Jim Potter & George Barris, 128 pages, 9 1/4x6 1/2 inches, black & white with color cover, 1957. Photo and technical stories on custom car building.

Left: Fawcett Publications: *Hot Rod Ideas*, by Griffith Borgeson & Wayne Thoms, 128 pages, 9 1/4x6 1/2 inches, black & white, 1961. Cover features Ed Roth with *Beatnik Bandit*. Super stock racing, street rods, and go-karts. Right: Ace: *Rod Builder Handbook*, 124 pages, 9 1/4x6 1/2 inches, black & white, 1961. Typical little book from a small publisher.

Petersen Publishing Trend Books: *Custom Show Cars*, by George Barris, 128 pages, 9 1/4x6 1/2 inches, black & white with color cover, 1959. Features some of the best-known customs of the 1950s. Photo and technical stories on custom car building.

Petersen Publishing Trend Books: *Custom Cars 1959 Annual*, by Jim Potter, 128 pages, 9 1/4x6 1/2 inches, black & white with color cover, 1959. Photo and technical stories on custom car building.

Left: Petersen Publishing Trend Books: *Restyle Your Car*, by George Barris & Jim Potter, 128 pages, 9 1/4x6 1/2 inches, black & white with color cover featuring Lyle Lake's custom Buick, circa 1957. Photo and technical stories on custom car building. Right: Petersen Publishing Trend Books: *Custom Cars 1958 Annual*, by Jim Potter & George Barris, 128 pages, 9 1/4x6 1/2 inches, black & white with color cover, 1958. Photo and technical stories on custom car building.

Left: Petersen Publishing Spotlite Books: *Custom Car Wheels & Lowering*, by George Barris, 64 pages, 8x5 inches, black & white with color cover, 1963. Features Tony Cardoza's Radical Cushenbery '59 Chevy. Filled with how-to photo stories. Right: Petersen Publishing Spotlite Books: *Custom Painting Techniques*, by George Barris, 48 pages, 8x5 inches, black & white with color cover, 1961. Features the *Jade Idol, Beatnik Bandit,* and Jimmy Cirovello's '59 Chevy. Photo and technical stories on custom painting.

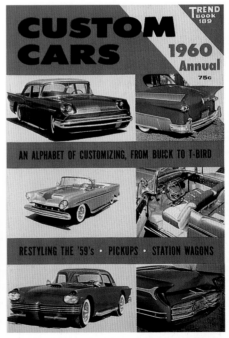

Petersen Publishing Trend Books: *Custom Cars 1960 Annual*, 128 pages, 9 1/4x6 1/2 inches, black & white with color cover, 1960. Photo and technical stories on custom car building.

Left: Petersen Publishing Spotlite Books: *Customizing Fins and Taillights*, by George Barris, 64 pages, 8x5 inches, black & white with color cover, 1961. How-to photo stories. Right: Petersen Publishing Spotlite Books: *Custom Headlights & Fenders*, by Hot Rod magazine editors, 64 pages, 8x5 inches, black & white with color cover, 1962. Photo and technical stories.

Petersen Publishing Trend Books: *Custom Cars 1961 Annual*, by George Barris, 128 pages, 9 1/4x6 1/2 inches, black & white with color cover, 1961. Features the Barris-built *Modern Grecian*. Photo and technical stories on custom car building.

Left: Petersen Publishing Spotlite Books: *Custom Upholstering*, by George Barris, 48 pages, 8x5 inches, black & white with color cover, 1962. How-to photo stories. Right: Petersen Publishing Spotlite Books: *Custom Dashboards and Detailing*, by George Barris, 64 pages, 8x5 inches, black & white with color cover, 1962. Photo and technical stories.

Petersen Publishing Trend Books: *Custom Cars 1962 Annual*, by George Barris, 128 pages, 9 1/4x6 1/2 inches, black & white with color cover, 1962. Features numerous customs including the Barris-built *X-Pack 400* air car, Tony Cardoza's '59 Chevy custom and Cushenbery's *Matador*. Photo and technical stories on custom car building.

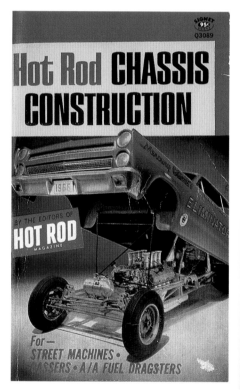

Petersen Publishing/Signet Books: *Hot Rod Chassis Construction*, 416 pages, 7x4 inches, paperback, photos and illustrations re-hashed from *Hot Rod* magazine. One of a series of books released by Signet.

Petersen Publishing/Signet Books: *Hot Rod Engines*, 416 pages, 7x4 inches, paperback, photos and illustrations re-hashed from *Hot Rod* magazine. One of a series of books released by Signet.

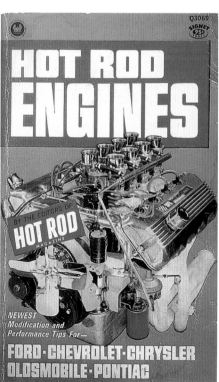

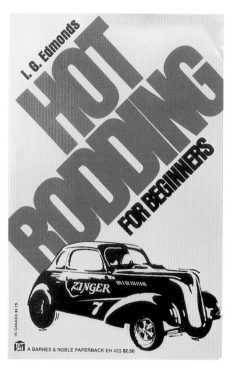

Barnes & Noble: *Hot Rodding For Beginners*, by I. G. Edmonds, 124 pages approx., 7x4 inches, paperback, circa 1972. Introduction to the sport of drag racing.

MAGAZINES

The most significant area of interest to hot rod memorabilia collectors is magazines and the Holy Grail of hot rodding has been the search to obtain a complete collection of original *Hot Rod* magazines. However, although *Hot Rod* is considered the pinnacle of magazines to collect, it was not the first hot rod magazine.

The first publications that promoted hot rods were newspapers such as *National Speedway Weekly* which covered roadster and hardtop speedway racers dating back to 1934. However, although rare, these newspapers are not highly prized by hot rod literature collectors as they contain only minor coverage of speedway and hardtop racing.

The first significant collectible hot rod magazine was *Throttle*, first published in 1941, which covered hot rods, racing, and high performance. *Throttle* lasted less than a year and closed down as the United States entered World War II, when its entire staff and readership were called to serve their country. *Speed Age* appeared in 1947 and followed much the same format as *Throttle*. It was also a great hot rod publication and lasted for many years. Today it is one of the most highly prized hot rod magazines to collect.

Hot Rod magazine made its debut in January 1948 with a street price of 25¢. IT featuring Eddie Hulse on the cover in his Southern California Timing Association's (SCTA) Class C winning track-nosed dry lakes roadster just after it had beaten the class record of 129.40 miles per hour.

Within a few years there were several magazines covering the expanding hot rod hobby. Some of them were on the market for a few issues only and

Right
Magazines are among the most popular hot rod collectibles. Some collectors specialize in first issues only, while others concentrate on accumulating all of the issues of a particular magazine.

Hot Rod: First issue January 1948, 22 pages. Featured Eddie Hulse on the cover in his winning SCTA Class C roadster. Most valuable, original, *Hot Rod* magazine. Reproductions available for under $10.

Hot Rod: Second issue February 1948, 22 pages. Featured Keith Landrigan's blue Class C SCTA roadster on the cover. Highly valued as an original issue. Reproductions available for under $10.

Hot Rod: Third issue March 1948, 22 pages. Featured Don Blair's '27 T on the cover. Highly valued as an original issue. Reproductions available for under $10.

Hop Up: First issue August 1951, 22 pages. A little book magazine covering hot rods, customs, boats, racing, and motorcycles from Enthusiasts' Publications. *Hop Up* changed its name in 1953 to *Motor Life*.

Speed: First issue November 1954, 22 pages. A pocket-sized little book, 4x5 1/2 inches, covering hot rods, customs, boats, racing, and planes. February 1953 issue shown.

Honk: First issue May 1953, 48 pages. A little book magazine covering custom cars and hot rods from Enthusiasts' Publications. In 1953 the *Honk* name was changed to *Car Craft* which continues today as one of the premier magazines in the street machine and drag racing world.

Speed Age: First issue May 1947, 22 pages. Offered a wide variety of stories on early high performance and racing activities worldwide. Published by Speed Age Inc., Maryland. January 1950 shown.

Throttle: First issue January 1941. Lasted only a year before the magazine closed up because of World War II. Published by Jack Peters. *Throttle* covered early dry lakes, speedway, and West Coast hot rodding. Rare.

others for just a few years. *Honk* changed its name to *Car Craft*, and it is still in production today, while *Hop Up*, first published in 1951 by the owners of *Road & Track*, Enthusiasts' Publications. Went through a metamorphosis in 1953 and reappeared as *Motor Life* and changing its focus to new production cars. It faded from the market in the mid-1960s.

The search for *Hot Rod* magazines has a two-fold attraction for many collectors, not only is it possible for them to acquire a complete collection, it is an enjoyable magazine, full of vintage hot rod technology, much of which still applies to the sport today. Early *Hot Rod*'s other great asset is its pictorial content which displays a wide range of hot rod photos, along with coverage of early drag racing, the dry lakes, and Bonneville. Surprisingly, *Road & Track* and *Motor Trend* also had extensive coverage of hot rods and custom cars in the late 1940s before they found their editorial direction in the automotive magazine business and took off after new cars and road racing.

As the 1950s sped forward hot rodding and custom car magazines spread into an amazing array of magazines. *Speed Mechanics* arrived in 1953 along with *Honk*, *Rod and Custom*, and *Sports Cars and Hot Rods*.

In November 1954, *Speed* magazine came onto the market followed by *Rodding and Restyling* in April 1955. *Rod Builder* began in July 1956 and *Hot Rod News* appeared in January 1957. *Northwest Rods* also debuted in January 1957. *Custom Rodder*, *Custom Cars*, and *Car Speed and Style* followed in December of the same year.

In June 1958, *Rods Illustrated* was published followed by *Customs Illustrated* in July. From Argus Publishers came *Popular Hot Rodding*, which entered the market in November 1962.

Argus Publishers was started by Don Warner, an ex-Petersen Publishing employee, and Gordon Baines, and grew to become the number two automotive publishing company in the country. Two of its hot rodding titles were *Popular Customs* and *Popular Hot Rodding*. *Popular Hot Rodding* continues to be published today. In 1995 Argus was purchased and combined with McMullen and Yee Publishing to form McMullen-Argus.

Street Rodder was started by Tom McMullen, an ex-Petersen freelance writer/photographer and hot rod builder in May 1972

Ray Brock, ex-editor of *Hot Rod* magazine, started *Rod Action* in August 1972. This magazine was sold to Challenge Publications and continues as a regular street rodding magazine.

A few short-lived hot rod magazines have appeared over the ensuing years but few have succeeded like the well-known magazines from Petersen, Argus and McMullen.

Two other notable magazines appeared in the mid-1960s, *American Rodding*, introduced by Popular Library Inc., an East Coast publisher, and *Modern Rod*, published by MPS on the West Coast. They did well for a time but both closed up within five years.

In 1987, two more magazines came onto the scene, *Hot Rod Mechanix* in June, and *American Rodder* in October. *Hot Rod Mechanix* was published by yet another ex-Petersen Publishing employee, LeRoi "Tex" Smith. Tex had worked as editor of *Hot Rod* but focused his new magazine on the home builder. *American Rodder* was a new publishing venture for Paisano Publications.

In the 1990s, *Rodder's Journal* appeared and has taken the road to success. It first appeared in 1994 and, with its superior high-quality production, has become a market leader. Its first issue became an instant collector's edition due to its short run of reverse printed covers.

Pricing: The low prices of magazines has made them easily obtainable to the collector and especially good value due to the added enjoyment of their content. Most early *Hot Rods* can be found for $10 to $25 although some early issues run as high as $100 to $200. The first issue of *Hot Rod* in fine shape can command up to $1,000. Other titles are more achievable with prices of $2 to $20. (The pricing of magazines on the East Coast is about half these figures.)

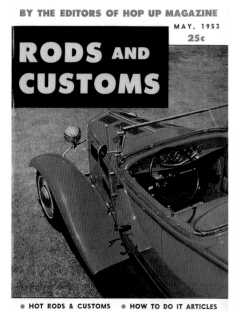

BY THE EDITORS OF HOP UP MAGAZINE

RODS AND CUSTOMS

MAY, 1953
25¢

● HOT RODS & CUSTOMS ● HOW TO DO IT ARTICLES
● TECHNICAL FEATURES ● A VARIETY OF PHOTOS

Rods and Customs: First issue May 1953, 44 pages. Name changed to *Rod and Custom* with the second issue.

Plymouth • Stude • Buick • Olds • Dodge • Cad • DeSoto • Lincoln

22 PAGES OF RARELY RESTYLED CARS!

September 1960
25¢
K

***Customs* ILLUSTRATED**

Mercur-dechrome!

**Get Rid of That Connie Kit
Do-It-Yourself Rag Top**

Bonus Features

**14 CHRYSLER TAIL-LIGHT TREATMENTS
DESIGNER'S IDEAS FOR CHEV REARS**

Customs Illustrated: First issue July 1958, 66 pages, 5x8 inches. A little book magazine from the East Coast covering mostly customs. September 1960 issue shown.

Rod Builder and Customizer: First issue July 1956, 66 pages, 5x8 inches. An East Coast little book covering rods and customs. September 1956 issue shown.

SPEED MECHANICS

AUTO RACES

JANUARY
25¢
ANC

**SO YOU WANT TO
BUILD A HOT ROD!!**

Speed Mechanics: First issue January 1953. This magazine lasted until the 1960s, from Hobby Publications in Maryland.

**ROD BUILDER
AND CUSTOMIZER**

SEPTEMBER 1956 25¢

**Build Your Own
$196 Sports Rod**

COMPLETE STEP BY STEP
BODY PLANS
AND SPECS

**Tips from
the Strips:**
ALL THE NEWEST
TRENDS IN
RODDING AND
CUSTOMIZING

Elvis Presley —
Rock 'N Roll Rodder

**AMERICA'S
NUMBER ONE
ROADSTER**

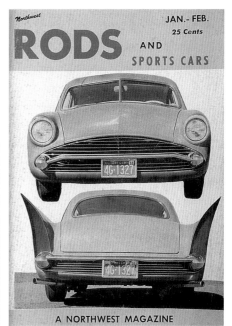

Northwest

RODS AND SPORTS CARS

JAN.- FEB.
25 Cents

A NORTHWEST MAGAZINE

Northwest Rods and Sports Cars: First issue October 1957, 44 pages, 5x8 inches. A little book from the Washington/Oregon area covering hot rods, customs, and sports cars. Originally entitled *Northwest Rods.*

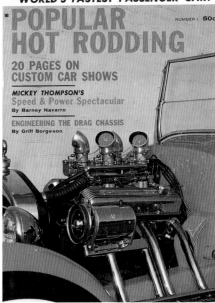

"WORLD'S FASTEST PASSENGER CAR!"

**POPULAR
HOT RODDING**

NUMBER 1 50¢

**20 PAGES ON
CUSTOM CAR SHOWS**

MICKEY THOMPSON'S
Speed & Power Spectacular
By Barney Navarro

ENGINEERING THE DRAG CHASSIS
By Griff Borgeson

Popular Hot Rodding: First issue November 1964, 64 pages, 8 1/2x11 inches. Originally published by the Argus Publishers Corporation, it is now part of McMullen-Argus.

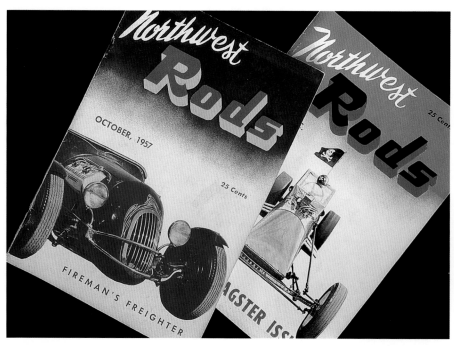

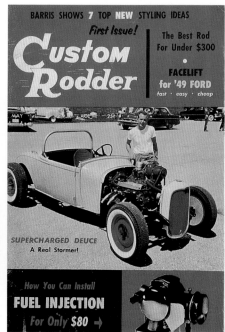

Northwest Rods: First issue October 1957, 44 pages, 5x8 inches. A little book from the Washington/Oregon area covering the hot rod scene. Later re-titled *Northwest Rods and Sports Cars*.

Custom Rodder: First issue December 1957, 44 pages, 5x8 inches. Published on the East Coast, covers hot rods and customs. First issue shown.

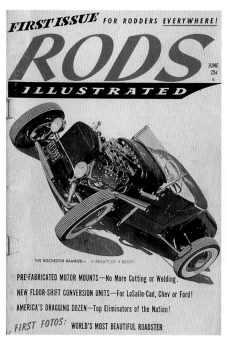

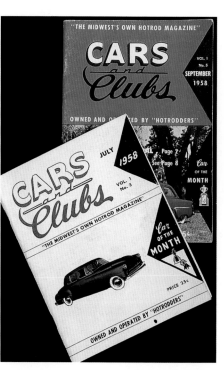

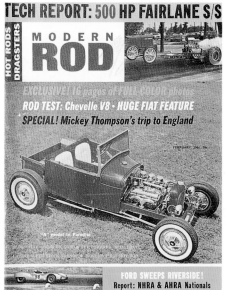

Rods Illustrated: First issue June 1958, 44 pages, 5x8. inches. Published on the East Coast, covers hot rods and customs. First issue shown.

Cars and Clubs: First issue May 1958, 22 pages, 5x8 inches. A little book magazine covering the hot rods and customs scene in the midwest. Cover noted that the magazine was "Owned and Operated by Hotrodders." July and September 1958 issues shown.

Modern Rod: First issue February 1964, 66 pages, 8 1/2x11 inches. Published on the West Coast by the MPS Corporation and covered hot rods, drag racing, and customs. Displayed some of the first high-quality color printing in hot rod magazines. First issue shown.

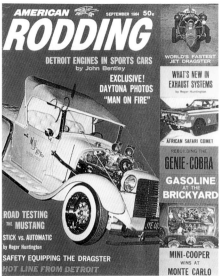

American Rodding: First issue September 1964, 70 pages, 8 1/2x11 inches. Published by Popular Library on the East Coast, covers hot rods, customs, and racing. Surprisingly, first issue carried no advertising. First issue shown.

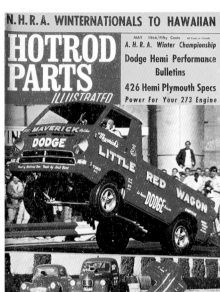

Hot Rod Parts Illustrated: First issue circa 1963, 70 pages, 8 1/2x11 inches. Published on the West Coast by Jack Chappell and covered drag racing and racing parts classified ads. May 1966 issue shown.

Ray Brock's Rod Action: First issue August 1972, 66 pages, 8 1/2x11 inches. Ray Brock was the publisher of *Hot Rod* magazine and left to form his own magazine, *Rod Action*. The magazine was later sold to Challenge Publications and is still in production.

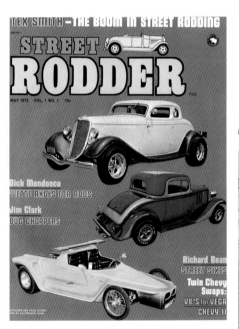

Street Rodder: First issue May 1972, 8 1/2x11 inches. Published by Tom McMullen in California and covered street rodding around the country. First issue shown.

Hot Rod Mechanix: First issue September 1987, 62 pages, 8 1/2x11 inches. New home builder hot rod magazine by Tex Smith featuring his famous rod project, "Dollar a pound rod," on the cover.

Streetrods Unlimited: First issue 1985, 60 pages, 8 1/2x11 inches. This only lasted three or four issues; a slick quality publication that failed to gain market share. Third issue shown.

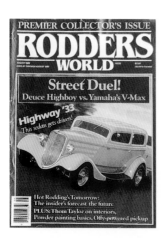

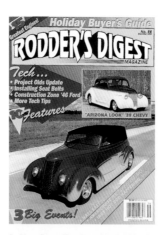

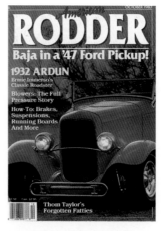

Rodders World: First issue August 1985, 78 pages, 8 1/2x11 inches. First issue shown. Inter-World Publications; no longer in print.

Rodder s Digest: First Issue March 1981, 72 pages, 8 1/2x11 inches. December 1993 issue shown. Produced as a quarterly, then as a bimonthly by Gerry Burger/Target Publications. Currently in print.

American Rodder: First issue October 1987, 78 pages, 8 1/2 x 11 inches. Produced by Paisano Publications and currently in print.

Popular Customs: First issue 1967, quarterly publication, 66 pages, 8 1/2x11 inches. Covered the custom car scene. Spring 1968 shown.

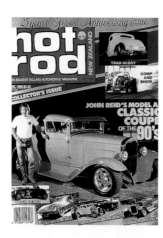

Custom Rodder: First issue Winter 1967, 50 pages, 8 1/2x11 inches. Australia s first hot rodding magazine, remained in print for 25 years. Published by Eddie Ford. January 1982 reprint edition shown.

Hot Rod New Zealand: First issue 1967, 44 pages, 8 1/2 x 11 inches. New Zealand s biggest-selling automotive magazine. 25th Silver Anniversary issue shown.

Sports Illustrated occasionally covered sports other than major ball sports. This April 24, 1961, issue features a couple of rodders looking over a T-bucket wearing original Roth airbrushed monster shirts. This same image appears on the hot rod record compilation *Wax Em Down!*

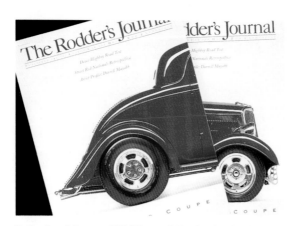

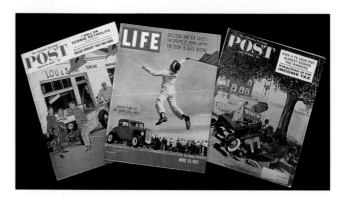

Rodder s Journal: First issue 1994, 128 pages, 9x11 inches. A perfect-bound art-stock magazine with little advertising, expensive, and worth every buck. Still in print. First issue shown, with collectors issue shown over the regular edition.

Saturday Evening Post and *Life* magazines featured great hot rod covers. The *Saturday Evening Post* covers are Norman Rockwell-style illustrations. Left is March 26, 1960, and right is July 13, 1961. The center panel is *Life* magazine, April 29, 1957; this is the classic hot rod drag racing image from the 1950s. These issues are rare and prized.

Collectors of paper hot rodding related material get a double bonus, especially with catalogs and programs as they feature historical information, unique vehicles, interesting products and some wonderful graphic images not found anywhere else.

Companies associated with hot rod and high performance parts in the past have generally printed catalogs or parts flyers from the beginning of their enterprise. They were usually simple little booklets of four to eight pages. Most of them did not have photos. An example is the very early Edelbrock catalogs. Their value now, as collectors' items, is first rate as the catalog are irreplaceable.

The sport of hot rodding blossomed in the beginning of the 1950s with a diversity of hot rodding activities such as speedway racing, the dry lakes, Bonneville, and street rodding. Due to these activities, many companies expanded quite rapidly in Southern California including Iskenderian, Edelbrock, Offenhauser, Moon, and Weiand. By the mid-1950s, they were issuing multi-page catalogs which were quite simple and illustrated with black and white photos and line drawings.

Along with company catalogs came speed shop catalogs from such famous shops as Alex Xydias' So-Cal Speed Shop in Burbank, California; Roy Reitcher's Bell Auto Parts in Bell, California; and Lee's Speed Shop in Oakland, California; they all sold their catalogs for 25¢ to 50¢ or gave them away.

Outside California, for 50¢ you could obtain multi-make performance parts catalogs from Almquist Engineering in Milford, Pennsylvania; Midwest Racing Equipment in Cleveland, Ohio; Honest Charley Speed Shop in Chattanooga, Tennessee; and Speed Parts in East Pattersen, New Jersey.

In Santa Fe Springs, California, Dean Moon's shop put out its first catalog around 1955 entitled *Moon*

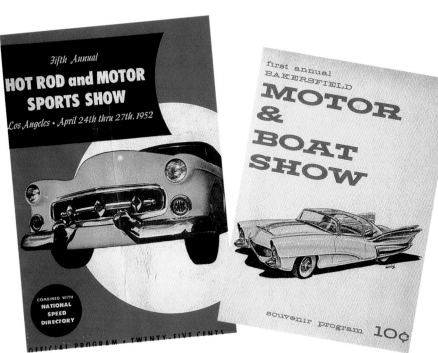

This program for the Fifth Annual Hot Rod and Motor Sports Show, April 1952, featured a custom Chevrolet on the cover.

The souvenir program from the first Bakersfield Motor & Boat Show cost 10¢. The cover featured a pencil illustration of the Barris-built *Golden Sahara* which appeared at the show.

The International Motor Sports Show in Hollywood is another George Barris-promoted show. This souvenir program showed the *Golden Sahara*.

These Hot Rod Show World programs are highly collectible as they are filled with color photography of wild International Championship Auto Show cars.

paper collecting. Gathering material from a special show or event is one way of creating a specific collection. An example is the Grand National Roadster Show in Oakland, California, which is almost 50 years-old and has many programs and souvenir promotional items.

The first hot rod shows at the Los Angeles Armory and the Urich/Gibb Lincoln-Mercury dealership in Whittier, California, produced programs and flyers and these are considered the rarest and most valuable of this kind of printed collectible.

Automotive which mixed with his own products a listing of parts from other manufacturers. It was a simple listing but within a short time he was publishing a 32-page *Fuel Systems & Accessories* catalog containing not just the parts he manufactured but technical tips, installation details, racing ideas, and a couple of good-looking girls to give the performance parts some extra appeal. Collectible custom car catalogs and flyers were issued by George Barris, Dean Jeffries, and Gene Winfield. This type of catalog thrived in the 1950s.

To cater to the expanding market, Edelbrock, Iskenderian, Moon, Bell, and Honest Charley Speed Shop, along with many others, started the mass marketing of hot rod and high performance parts by mail. This new method of selling increased sales as companies could now reach buyers who did not have a local speed equipment retailer. This burst of growth encouraged an all-out race to produce even better catalogs. Color catalogs entered the scene in about 1960, first with bright photos on the covers only and subsequently with four-color interior pages. These catalogs are a gold mine of information for anyone interested in the history of hot rod parts and accessories.

J.C. Whitney in Chicago, Illinois, issued a huge mail order catalog for auto parts listing a variety of hot rodding, high performance and custom car items. The price for their catalog was $1, an expensive item at the time, but it was refunded on the first $5 order. This catalog is still produced on a regular basis.

Specialization is a way of focusing in the field of

Rod and custom car shows flourished in the early 1950s across the country. Each state had a diverse collection of printed show programs and there were many promoters. Significant players on the West coast included George and Shirley Barris, who produced a program for each event they promoted: a series of custom and hot rod shows reaching almost the width and breadth of California.

In the 1960s, the International Championship Auto Shows Series were created by Bob Larivee's Promotions Inc. Bob took a succession of cars around the nation with dozens of show programs between 1960 and 1980. When street rodding flourished, local promoters like Blackie Gejeian in Fresno, California, and national promoters like the NSRA and Goodguys, continued this show program concept.

Collecting programs is similar to collecting trade catalogs. They are about the same size, but generally only run to 10 or 20 pages. Many are black and white with a two-color cover and later programs featured color covers.

Pricing is comprehensive and varied depending upon the condition of the catalog. Inaugural show programs run as high as $150 while those from the later 1950s' are $10 to $50. For a 1960s catalog, the price is $10; for the 1970s, it ranges from $5 to $8; later ones are around $5. More common mid-1950s programs are roughly $25, late 1950s and early 1960s are $15 to $25, and 1970s and 1980s programs are $5 to $10.

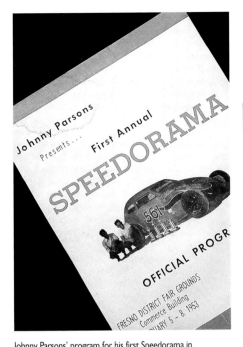

Johnny Parsons' program for his first Speedorama in Fresno in February 1953.

Harry Costa promoted this program for the 1961 San Mateo Custom, Rod & Sports Car Show. It consisted of 31 pages and featured "Loads of Pictures," including a Hurst technical section on engine swapping. The cover displays a photo of Tony Dow, "Wally" from the *Leave it to Beaver* show.

The 1964 souvenir program for the Grand National Roadster Show featured Dean Jeffries' fabulous *Manta Ray* on the cover and sold for 50¢.

Harry Costa's San Mateo Auto Show Car Show Album was a multipage photo presentation which strangely featured a pen drawing of a jet airplane.

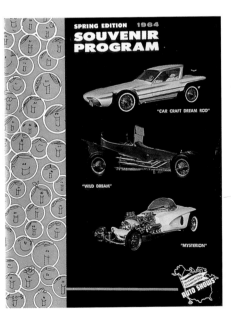

This 1964 souvenir program from the International Championship Auto Show was one of the first to feature a color cover. It showed the *Car Craft Dream Rod*, Joe Wilhelm's *Wild Dream*, and Ed Roth's strange twin-engined *Mysterion*. These programs were re-used at many shows as these cars toured in a group.

Seattle's British Automobile Show must have been an unusual event as the cover of the program featured stock cars, the new *Mustang Dragster*, and Gene Winfield's *Reactor*.

The 1969 Sacramento Autorama Souvenir Program showed the Barris-built *Coach* for Paul Revere and the Raiders. This wild twin-Pontiac-powered machine toured the country. It's a pity the lads aren't around.

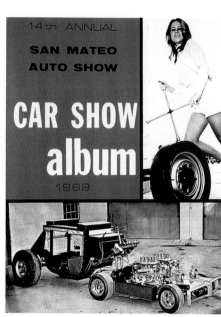

Harry Costa mixed love and lust on the cover of his San Mateo Auto Show's Car Show Album with a beautiful young lady and Barris' Raiders' *Coach*. This is a multipage presentation and well worth collecting.

The Grand National Roadster Show souvenir program from 1974 displayed the previous year's winner, Chuck Corsello's T-bucket, on the cover.

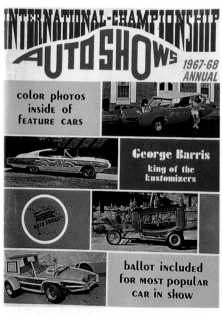

This is the International Championship Auto Shows' first full color program. The 1967/1968 annual featured Dean Jeffries' *Monkeemobile* along with George Barris' *Thunder Charger,* the *Calico Surfer,* and Farhner's *Boothill Express.* By 1980, the program had expanded to 140 pages, with 82 of the pages in color, and Promotions Inc. was selling over 300,000 of them annually.

This rare program from the Sabers Car Club in Denver, Colorado, for their 12th auto exhibition featured a replica of the 1934 Bonnie & Clyde Ford and Richard Korkes-built *Batcycle,* which George Barris toured around the country.

Blackie Gejeian has been the promoter of the Fresno Autorama Show for many years. His official souvenir program featured an illustration of the Joe Bailon-built six-engine *Snakemobile.*

In 1966, the International Championship Auto show's souvenir program featured a wildly colorful cover with Barris' *Surf Woody* and *Munster Coach*, Roth's *Surfite* and Casper's *Ghost*.

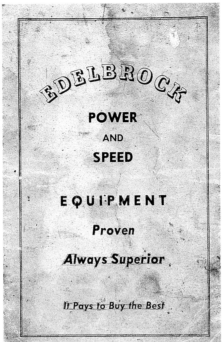

This early Edelbrock Power and Speed Equipment catalog from around 1950 gave a simple list of parts available from the company. Vic, Sr., noted on the catalog, "It pays to buy the best." He proved his point; today Edelbrock is one of the biggest and best high performance manufacturers in the industry.

PLEASE NOTE
IMPORTANT DETAILS
ON LAST PAGE
OF THIS PRICE LIST

FOR POLISHED EQUIPMENT, SEE SPECIAL SECTION AT END OF PRICE LIST.

Offenhauser was an early high performance parts manufacturer who built his reputation at Indy and on the dirt speedways of America. This ultra-rare 1954 general catalog of about 20 pages of lists reminded the buyer that Offenhauser was "The Perfect Combination."

Moon's first comprehensive catalog was a 32-page booklet issued in early 1955. It offered tanks, valves, fuel blocks, carburetors, and a mass of small high performance parts.

Almquist Engineering put out a mass of excellent high performance directory catalogs. This 1957/58 edition offered everything for the hot rodder to build a wild machine.

Lee's Speed Shop manufactured the Tornado V-8 valve-in-head conversion for flathead Fords. Their catalog from 1953 featured a sprint car fitted with one of their conversions. This multipage catalog is a classic for its time. Rare and highly collectible.

Bell Auto Parts, under the guidance of Roy Richter, became one of the biggest hot rod and high performance parts shops in California. This catalog from around 1948 has great illustrations by Gus Maanum of a roadster and a sprint car.

Honest Charley Speed Shop opened house in 1948. This 10th anniversary edition of his hand-drawn catalog in 1958 shows that Charley kept a low-buck operation and passed low pricing onto his customers.

Bell Auto Parts, Inc. progressed to become "the Big Name in Racing Equipment." Based in Bell, California, they developed the Bell Helmet which is featured on the cover of Catalog No. 33.

Almquist Engineering from Milford, Pennsylvania, started as a mail order high performance parts distributor just after World War II. By 1962, they had grown to become the "World's Largest Supplier of Hi-Performance Equipment." Their thick catalog sold for 25¢ a copy.

Weber Tool Company, a high performance parts manufacturer, was one of the 1950s' and 1960s most popular choices for valve train and clutch assemblies. This catalog was published around 1962.

This exceedingly rare Summers Brothers' Golden Rod press release folder was filled with press material on their 409.277-miles per hour world land speed record.

Juvenile literature introduced many young boys to hot rods while improving their reading skills at the same time. Hot rodding books in the school library encouraged slow readers; they read and re-read the works of authors such as Henry Gregor Felson, Robert Bowen, and William Campbell Gault. Maybe it wasn't great English literature but for the readers it was as good as Steinbeck and Thoreau. It has been noted by school librarians and teachers that the small books of *Hot Rod*, *Rag Top*, and *Drag Strip* helped a generation of young men (gearheads) get on with their education.

Henry Felsen was a professional writer who had served as a drill instructor in the U.S. Marine Corps during World War II. He later served as a roving editor for *Leatherneck* magazine, wrote movie screen-plays, approximately three dozen books, and created material for network television. His classic works were six hot rod books he wrote for kids and they have become famous among male-focused juvenile literature.

In July 1950, E.P. Dutton published Felsen's book called *Hot Rod* as a hardback. The company's main marketing was to schools and in the following 10 years, nine editions of *Hot Rod* were printed. In 1951, trade paperback editions were licensed to Bantam who proceeded, over the next 20 years, to reprint them 21 times. Bantam also picked up the trade paperback rights to the other Felsen hot rod books.

With this many editions of a single book it's not too hard to locate the different print runs of *Hot Rod*. Felsen's other books also had some significant print runs: *Rag Top* (1954-first edition) was printed twice by Random House and twice by Bantam, *Street Rod* (1954-first edition) was printed 13 times by Random

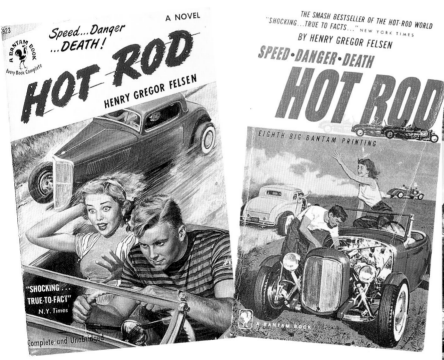

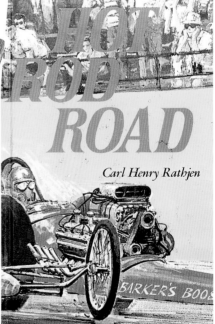

Felsen's *Hot Rod* was reprinted 21 times by Bantam Books, making it the all-time biggest seller of its kind about hot rods. This book was Henry Gregor Felsen at his best, spinning tales of wild hot rod adventures. The great cover art is an added plus. Paperback, 181 pages, 1951.

Bantam must have been pleased with *Hot Rod* as they bannered this paperback edition as the "Eighth Big Bantam Printing." Fresh art was added to the cover that was vibrant and exciting. Paperback, 153 pages, 1958.

Hot Rod Road by Carl Henry Rathjen was a tale of wild drag racing and hot rods, in the Felsen tradition. Great cover art helped this book along. Hardback library edition, 1968.

House and 23 times by Bantam, *Fever Heat* (1954-first edition) was printed once by Angus Vicker and once by Fawcett, *Crash Club* (1958-first edition) was printed twice by Random House and 17 times by Bantam. Felsen's last hot rod book *Road Rocket* (1960-first edition) was printed four times by Random House and 12 times by Bantam.

In 1990, GP/Books issued a limited run of 2,500 collector sets of the six books as trade paperbacks with a slipcase titled *The Henry Gregor Felsen Collection*. This is worth having as it pulls all the Felsen books into one set with great cover art from artists including Bill Neale, Bruce Kaiser, Rich Boyd, Steve Pasteiner, and Ken Eberts.

Felsen's series is worth collecting as a first edition set. They are also fun for hot rodders to read for the first time and for folks who read them in high school they will no doubt enjoy reading them again. These school library editions are the most common because of the volume of reprints totaling over 115 editions.

Many editions of *Hot Rod* have great art on their slipcovers. Some of the school library editions have hot rod images printed directly onto the cover. One collector has eleven different covers to Felsen's *Hot Rod* and he believes that the total may well be more than 25.

Some of the writers who followed in Felsen's footsteps were William Campbell Gault, Patrick O'Connor, Philip Harkins, and Robert Sidney Bowen. William Campbell Gault wrote *Drag Strip*, *Speedway Challenge*, and *Thunder Road*; Patrick O'Connor wrote *Mexican Road Race* and *Black Tiger at Le Mans*; Philip Harkins wrote *A Day at the Drag Race*. Robert Sidney Bowen's work is lesser known but he was a productive author who wrote more than 20 books. His hot rod related books included *Hot Rod Outlaws*, *Hot Rod Angels*, *Hot Rod Patrol*, *Hot Rod Rodeo*, *Hot Rod Showdown*, and *Dirt Track Danger*. His works were mostly published by the Chilton Book Company.

Most of these books were published as a mixture of hardback and trade paperbacks with great cover art of hot rods and racing cars caught in action. They were sold as 60¢ scholastic trade paperbacks published under the Highland Books banner by Berkley Publishing.

The Felsen books followed a formula, informing youth of the dangers of street racing and acting stupid behind the wheel of an automobile. The works of Gault and Harkins did much the same but added money and a little more lust and love to these simple stories. In the 1970s, movies such as George Lucas' *American Graffiti* spun off a trade paperback of the same name.

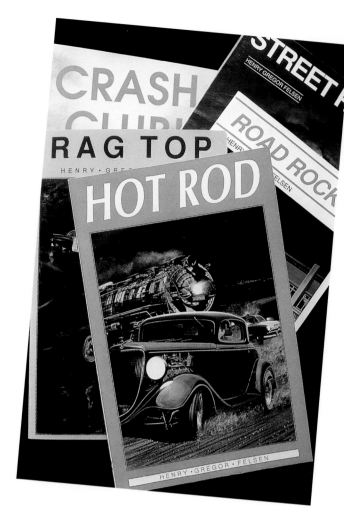

This is the latest collectors' set of Henry Gregor Felsen's hot rod books. The set of six sold for $35 and only 2,500 sets were printed.

A series of juvenile-directed books, which appeared in the late 1960s, were technically focused but printed as small sized paperbacks, with as many as 416 pages. Petersen Publishing licensed The New American Library in New York to publish through their Signet Books division several thick paperback books filled with technical information and stories about hot rodding, engine building, and racing. The information was condensed from past issues of *Hot Rod* magazine as a series of how-to books including: *How to Build Hot Rods*, *Super Tuning*, and *Hot Rod Chassis Construction*. They were sold for 95¢.

The small trade paperbacks trend to publish hot rod books continued with *The Hot Rod Handbook* (1957 and 1965) from the American Sports Library, and *Dragging and Driving* (1965) from Scholastic Book Services.

These books are inexpensive and are fun to collect. Trade paperbacks sell for $1 to $5 while old high school hardback editions of Felsen and others sell from $5 to $15. The Felsen Collectors' editions sold for about $35 new and can still be found for about that price.

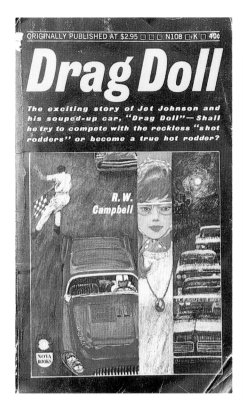

Drag Doll from the pen of R. W. Campbell was a tale of love, lust, fast cars, and quite a bargain too. Nova Books, 1963.

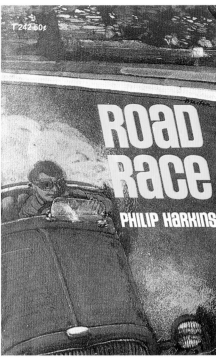

Philip Harkins turned out quite lot of short story books including *The Day of the Drag Race* and *Road Race*. This edition of *Road Race* featured an aero-screened roadster tearing down the road. Another great bargain at 50¢. Scholastic Book Services, 1961.

Bantam published Felsen's *Crash Club* 17 times and one edition featured this great watercolor image of a Corvette heading for a '34 Ford coupe. The lady looks like she is about to abandon the car. 202 pages, 1963 edition.

William Campbell Gault wrote *Drag Strip* in the mid-1950s and added a little more lust to the subject while retaining a wild story line about hot rodders living on the edge. Published by E.P. Dutton, 1958.

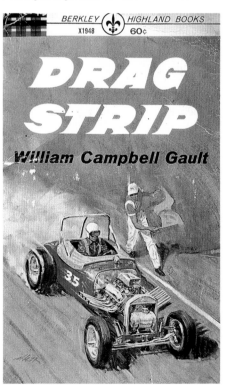

This paperback edition of *Drag Strip* was published by Berkley Highland Books in 1959 with super watercolor artwork of an altered roadster. Gault also wrote *Thunder Road* and a *Speedway Challenge*.

This collectors' edition of *Street Rod* by Henry Gregor Felsen features a great painting by Jack Juratovic and is the 36th edition of the book since 1953. Published by GP books.

STREET WAS FUN IN '51

Albert Drake

Street Was Fun in '51—this great book by long-time hot rod journalist and historian Albert Drake is a must for any collection. Still in print and worth every cent. Drake also wrote *Flat Out* which is another must. Flat Out Press, 1982.

Dragging and Driving by Tom MacPherson published by Scholastic Book Services in 1960 covered the hot rod hobby and the dangers of bad driving. Find out what a Johnson Rod is! To find out the answer, get a copy just for fun.

American Graffiti by George Lucas and co-written by Gloria Katz and Willard Huyck asked, "Where were you in '62?" *American Graffiti* spun a tale about cruisin', hot rodders, girls, and fun in the early 1960s. Worth finding.

Since comic books were invented, they've had a tremendous audience. Usually they have been fun to read because of inventive storylines and great illustrations. By the 1950s, comic books were an obsession for young and old alike, offering an amazing variety of heroes including Batman, The X-Men, Spider-man, The Flash, The Silver Surfer, and Superman.

Hot rodders weren't forgotten. Comic publishers introduced Clint Curtis, Scott Jackson, and Ken King and the Boys through the medium of comics.

Clint Curtis debuted in November 1951 in *Hot Rod Comics,* which was published by Fawcett Publications of Greenwich, Connecticut. After six issues the rights to the comic were sold to Charlton Comics. Right on Fawcett's heels in competition was Hillman Periodicals who introduced *Hot Rod and Speedway* in February 1952, but this comic only lasted five issues

and its publication ceased in April 1953. *Hot Rod King* was another hot rod comic title published by Ziff-Davis in the fall of 1952, but it had an even shorter life, lasting only one issue.

Fawcett's title of *Hot Rod Comics* was too centered for Charlton so the comic was renamed *Hot Rods and Racing Cars* in hopes of gaining a wider audience. *Hot Rods and Racing Cars* lasted from November 1951 until June 1973 and totaled 120 issues. Overlapping this title was *Hot Rod Racers* which was introduced in December 1964 and lasted 15 issues until July 1967.

Speed Demons was added to the list of growing Charlton CDC bimonthly comic titles. The comics fed the reader a steady tale of hot rodders living on the edge, building and driving fast cars, chasing girls, living high, and beating up the occasional guy who got out of line. For most readers, Clint was the hero they

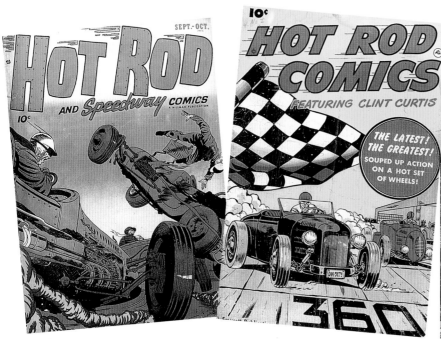

The *Hot Rod and Speedway Comics* from Hillman Periodicals lasted five issues. Its publication ceased in April 1953 following its introduction in February 1952. Very rare and a gem to find.

Clint Curtis debuted in November 1951 in *Hot Rod Comics*, published by Fawcett Publications, but after six issues the rights to the comic were sold to Charlton Comics. This edition is one of the first from Fawcett and hard to find. Its price was 10¢, quite a bargain as this comic had great cover art right from the start.

Hot Rods and Racing Cars' new look included this wild looking art-work designed with a cog and gear, nut and bolt logo. Issue #17.

admired, a kind of allaround nice guy who liked to drive fast and hang out. For mothers who glanced at what their teenage sons spent hours reading, Clint was a sociopathic lawbreaker who encouraged teenagers to drive too fast and live too wild.

From the beginning, *Hot Rod Comics* were in vivid color and printed on pulp newsprint. Unfortunately the newsprint had a high acid level which caused the paper to yellow and eventually self-destruct. However, if the comic was stored out of the sunlight, away from chemical vapors, and at a suitable humidity level, it remained in a surprisingly good and readable condition. The comics that have badly deteriorated are hardly worth collecting, they fall apart and leave the collector out of pocket, with a mess to clean up, too.

The covers of *Hot Rod Comics* were printed on a quality coated paper stock with much finer printing qualities and more colorful inks. In the beginning they featured special cover artwork, but later issues of *Hot Rods and Racing Cars* featured panels and images from the stories inside the issue. Early issues also offered car-care stories and tech tips on how cars worked, similar to regular automotive magazines.

Surprisingly, Clint Curtis wasn't a good-looking guy, but oh, how he could drive! Hot rods, dragsters, land speed race cars, NASCAR sedans and speedway jalopies—Clint was the all-American boy racer with the abilities of Mario Andretti, Craig Breedlove, Johnny Rutherford and "Fireball" Roberts. What is also interesting to gather from the comic stories is that he had no visible means of support but, boy, did he ever have a most amazing lifestyle!

Over the years his chiseled looks improved, and in his redesign he lost some of the ape-ish look that he had in the earlier issues. The initial illustrations for *Hot Rods* were delightfully penned by Joe Shuster and Ray Osrin. In the 1960s, illustrators Jack Keller and Nicholas Alascia helped create *Hot Rod and Racing Cars*, *Hot Rod Racers*, *Drag N' Wheels*, and *Drag-Strip Hotrodders*. It is interesting to look at the art in the comic books and note how creatively the panels were drawn. The artists used an enormous variety of picture angles, with the cars accurately drawn and scaled even while surviving impossible stunts.

Most of the time the story lines were similar to the themes in hot rod movies showing at the same time in local theaters. The writers of the comics could well have been the scriptwriters for many of the movies such as *Drag Strip Girl* and *Ghost of Dragstrip Hollow*.

Charlton CDC Comics added more titles, and sales of the comics expanded to Europe, England, and Australia. *Top Eliminator*, with Scott Jackson and the

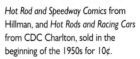

Hot Rod and Speedway Comics from Hillman, and *Hot Rods and Racing Cars* from CDC Charlton, sold in the beginning of the 1950s for 10¢.

Hot Rods and Racing Cars was Charlton's re-hashed title for *Hot Rod Comics*. The artwork was fresh, not taken from the inside panels, and displayed dramatic action on the cover of every issue.

Rod Masters, was introduced around 1962 while *Teenage Hotrodders*, *Drag N' Wheels*, *World of Wheels*, and *Grand Prix* comics were gradually introduced over the succeeding years. In June 1973 Charlton CDC Comics stopped producing the *Hot Rod Comic* series and today these rare editions are a wonderful memento of what folks imagined hot rodding to be at that time.

There were other comic books, most of them not as seriously focused as the Hot Rod Comic series. Petersen Publishing, who had been running cartoons, mostly drawn by Tom Medley, in *Hot Rod*, *Honk*, *Car Craft*, and *Rod & Custom*, introduced a new comic book in 1959. It was called *CARtoons* and featured delightful black and white drawings with a mixture of cartoons, games, photoplays, and funny car drawings.

CARtoons' impact was helped by great illustrations from Dave Deal, George Trosley, Mike Streff, Steve Austin, and Dennis Ellefson who contributed to *CARtoons* for many years. Ed Roth created his own line of comics with his Rat Fink character and has produced a variety of comics over the years.

The pricing of Charlton CDC *Hot Rod Comics* is hard to gauge but swap meets and dealer prices range from 50¢ to $15 depending upon vintage. First issues from Fawcett, Hillman and Ziff-Davis can draw prices of up to $75. Petersen Publishing's *CARtoons* runs from $1 to $5. Ed Roth's *Rat Fink* cartoon books price at $4 to $25 depending on their age.

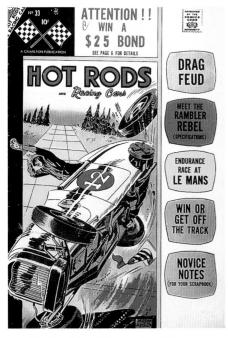

Issue #33 of *Hot Rods and Racing Cars* from 1955 featured approximately 70 pages of action, and judging by the cover, it was wild as could be, with an out-of-control roadster jumping about the place.

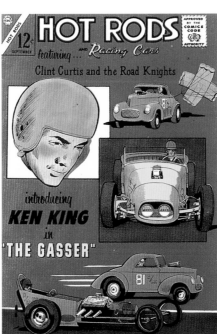

Into the 1960s, *Hot Rods and Racing Cars* evolved with new artwork and a more handsome Clint Curtis. Ken King also appeared as a new character. Tough, rugged, and fast like Curtis, King could drive anything on wheels.

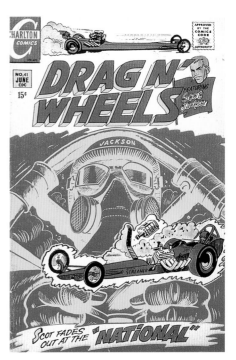

Drag N' Wheels was a fresh title from CDC in the 1960s and featured another new character, Scott Jackson. Like King and Curtis, Jackson was a man of machines who could drive like a bat out of hell. Issue #41.

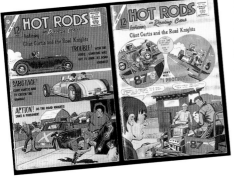

The story lines in both these issues of *Hot Rods and Racing Cars* played out some social morals with action using cool street rods or drag machines. As usual, Clint was a kind of "Mr. Clean."

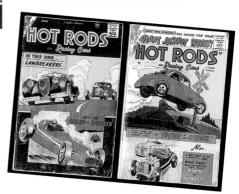

The May 1959 edition of *Hot Rods and Racing Cars* was all action as was the other issue with "Champ at Morocco" and "Lawbreakers." Both issues ran 32 pages, and it is notable that the illustration techniques improved vastly since the comic came on the market in 1951.

Left: The much later *Drag N' Wheels* #59, which was close to the last issue published, was rebannered with the Charlton logo in the early 1970s. Right: The August 1955 edition of *Hot Rods and Racing Cars* was bannered as a CDC comic.

Top

Hot Rod Racers took over from *Hot Rods and Racing Cars* in the 1970s as interest in hot rod comics started fading. The price hadn't gone up much in years but the page count slid to 24 pages, and although the cost had inched up to 12¢, it was still a bargain.

Bottom

Hot Rod Cartoons took over from *CARtoons* in the 1970s, evolving over the years with new illustrators such as Thompson, Lemmons, and Steefenhagen. A Petersen Publication.

CARtoons by Millar and Kohler was popular right from the start. These early issues were actually very funny and featured great penmanship and artistic styling from a couple of cartoon illustrators. This was the comic book where illustrators got their first breaks and some made good including, Dave Deal, George Trosley, Mike Streff, Steve Austin, and Dennis Ellefson. *CARtoons* became a Petersen title and continued for many years.

Top

The artwork in *Hot Rods and Racing Cars* and *Drag N' Wheels* became far more graphic in the mid-1960s. This pair of covers show dramatic scenes clipped from the stories inside.

Bottom

During the 1960s, *Hot Rod Cartoons* mirrored what was appearing in *Hot Rod* magazine, including the van and truck craze, along with buggies and four-wheel drives, with cartoons for everyone.

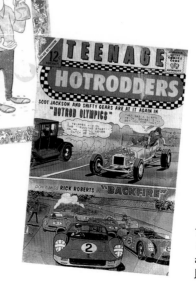

Teenage Hotrodders, a new Charlton title in the early 1960s, noted that Scott Jackson and Shifty Gears are at it again in "Hotrod Olympics." Nicholas Alascia and Jack Keller contributed great artwork for this comic.

This *Rat Fink Comix* is #4 in a small run of 32-page comics which Ed Roth published at the beginning of the 1990s. They are already collectors' items with a mix of hot rod-toons, sci-fi, and other weird stuff. As Rat Fink says on the cover, "Mazooma! A Fun Filled Issue."

With movies titles like *The Devil on Wheels*, *Dragstrip Riot*, *Hot Rod Gang*, and *Hot Rod Rumble*, it's not surprising that hot rodding had such a bad name in the 1950s. These movies portrayed an image of a gang mentality that really didn't exist in the way it was portrayed by Hollywood on the silver screen.

The poster for *Dragstrip Riot* screamed "MURDER . . . AT 120 MILES PER HOUR!" *Hot Rod Gang* was bannered "CRAZY KIDS . . . LIVING TO A WILD ROCK N' ROLL BEAT!"

Collecting movie posters and lobby cards is a fast-growing hobby and there is a variety of material available. However, there is a second, aesthetic, side to the collecting of this material. Many early posters were colorfully created with excellent traditional watercolor poster artwork and this has become prized by collectors of "Americana."

The most collectable of these movie posters used twisted messages to attract patrons to the movie. The posters fostered the idea that hot rodders were madmen who lived by murder, speed, and lust. It was Hollywood at its worst, exposing society's fascination and fear of "these disgusting hot rodders." It was a perfect image to go with the McCarthyism of the period.

Posters for movies like *High School Confidential* did not feature hot rods, but the story characterized the image of wild hot rodders street racing and chasing girls. The poster for *Hot Rod Gang* was wildly graphic with a painted scene of George Barris's car *Ala Kart* drag racing a '29 roadster while a beautiful young woman, Judy Farr, portrayed with huge pointed breasts and a minuscule waist, screamed in fear as rock star, Gene Vincent, rocked away in the background. This movie was produced before any kind of nudity was permissible in films and the poster carried the desired sexual image of lust and wild hot rodding. This *Hot Rod Gang* poster is now one of the

Right

Hot Rod Gang: These lobby cards from the movie are some of the most highly collectible of all hot rod movie lobby cards. They're colorful, detailed, and oh, so busty. 1958

The Devil on Wheels: The first classic teenage hot rod movie with street racing and some neat lobby cards. This card shows how hot rods really were back in the 1940s. No billet here! 1947.

Hot Rod: This is one of the lobby cards for *Hot Rod* and uses the same artwork and similar images as the poster. 1950.

Hot Rod: An original hot rod movie. This single sheet is in pristine condition, not mounted, but framed. The movie starred James Lydon and Gloria Winters. 1950.

Teen Age Thunder: This lobby card has drama, wild teenage love and lust, and squealing hot rods. Circa 1958.

Rebel Without a Cause: This single-sheet poster is classic James Dean, very rare and expensive, however, reproductions are available. It's a neat poster for a movie history buff as well as the crash-and-burn movie fan. 1955.

most desirable of all hot rod movie posters. Older guys remember it with a wonderful glow, and younger ones are delighted by the imagery.

According to Ron Main, a movie and poster dealer from "Main Attraction" in Canoga Park, California, many movie posters have survived in good condition as they were printed on quality poster paper with a coated front surface. He notes most posters and lobby cards have been stored out of the light so they show little UV deterioration.

Two styles of posters are being collected: full-sized ones, which come in four different sizes, and lobby cards. The poster sizes are: Insert, 14x36 inches, vertical; Half-Sheet: 28x22 inches, horizontal; One-Sheet: 27x41 inches, vertical; and Three-Sheet: 41x81 inches, vertical. Lobby cards measure 11x14 inches, vertical. The Half-Sheet and One-Sheet posters were displayed outside movie theaters in glass cases to attract customers to the ticket window. Interestingly, some of these larger posters can also be found in French and Spanish.

The Three-Sheet posters were used on outside billboards, placed in window boxes on the front of movie theaters. Unfortunately some were pasted into place with water-based glues so the only existing original Three-Sheets are those that were either never installed or were pinned or clipped into window boxes. Therefore, Three-Sheet posters are quite rare.

The problem with Three-Sheets for most collectors is their size—not many folks have space to display a 4x7 foot poster. This size problem is solved by collecting One-Sheet posters, which were generally just a reduction of the Three-Sheet poster's image. They are now the most sought after by both the specialized and general interest collectors.

Another interesting angle on poster collecting is that some movies had multiple posters. *Hot Rod*, which starred James Lydon, had at least three posters, all with different art. Some posters used a variety of images, and others, like *Hot Rod Gang*, used the same art but assembled it differently for each size of poster. The movies *Hot Rod Girl* and *Hot Car Girl* are often confused as they were both about the same subject—fast cars and wild women. Both the posters were colorful with painted images of wild car stunts and girls going crazy.

The second level of movie poster collecting is lobby cards and window cards. Both these types of movie posters are printed on cardboard stock rather than poster newsprint. Lobby cards are more common while windows cards are very rare. Virtually all windows cards were printed in black and white and measure 14x22 inches.

Lobby cards represent a far better value than window cards as they are almost always printed in

Running Wild: This great poster of curvaceous Mamie Van Doren is especially popular with collectors. "Teen-age . . . tough and tempted!" bannered this one-sheet poster. 1955.

four-color, although some, like those for *The Choppers*, were printed in two-color.

The first movie to feature street hot rods was the 1947 PRC Pictures production of *The Devil on Wheels*, starring Noreen Nash, Darryl Hickman, and James Cardwell. This movie has several classic lobby cards featuring the movie's street racing roadsters. Because they are the first, they are therefore the most collectible of hot rod lobby cards.

Lobby cards were displayed inside theaters to give patrons an impression of a current or upcoming attraction. The photos they showed were always from the wildest or most romantic part of the movie.

Later, hot rod-related movies like *American Graffiti* featured a mixture of art and photography. Unfortunately *American Graffiti* does not have a slick poster to remind us of the hot rod fun in the movie. Other printed movie collectibles include scripts, press books, and press kits. These make an interesting addition to any collection that is movie oriented rather than art directed.

Pricing for posters varies with the movie and the poster's popularity. Insert and Half-Sheets are $50 to $200; One-Sheets are $100 to $400; Three-Sheets run between $250 and $600. Lobby cards are the best value at $10 to $40 if the card has hot rods on it. Movie scripts generally run from $20 to $250.

Running Wild: This Half-Sheet poster mixed photography with art-work and was taken from the one-sheet Running Wild poster to create a new look.

Hot Car Girl: A highly collectible half-sheet poster. The art-work is an adaptation of the one-sheet image. The poster features Frank Monteleone's Barris-built 1956 Ford convertible. Frank still owns this car. 1956.

Drag Strip Girl: This full-sheet poster portrayed love and lust at speed. A seducible young woman and wild drag racing create a memorable image. 1956.

Hot Rod Girl: It's understandable that Lori Nelson went wild in this movie with "Teen-Age Terrorists burning up the streets!" This great lobby card is a rich and colorful must for any collection. 1958.

High School Confidential: This movie features some wild street racing, but unfortunately, the lobby card doesn't show a hint of the Barris-built Chevy customs or the hot rods that are in the movie. 1958.

Hot Rod Gang: This movie has so many variations on its posters and lobby cards that it makes up its own collection. The stunning image of a busty Jody Fair screaming as Gene Vincent rocks while the Barris-built *Ala Kart* screeches by, is hard to forget. 1958.

Hot Rod Rumble: This One-Sheet poster from Allied Artists mixed illustration and photography into a dramatic presentation. 1957.

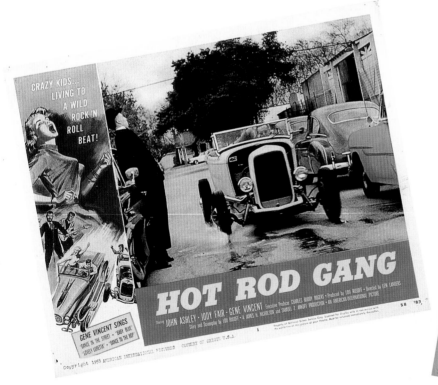

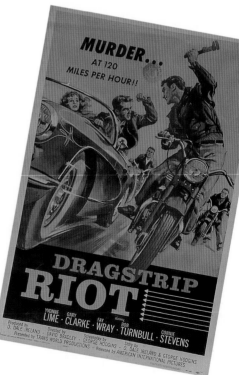

Hot Rod Gang: This lobby card is as bold as the posters and just as colorful. The movie has a large collection of lobby cards and Jody Fair's chest points the way on each one. 1958.

Dragstrip Riot: "Murder . . . at 120 Miles Per Hour!!" as bikers and hot rodders in Corvettes battle it out. Great action poster. 1958.

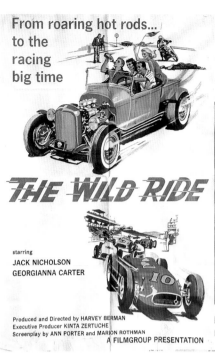

The Wild Ride: This full-sheet poster features a great roadster pickup and an image from Indy. "From roaring hot rods . . . to the racing big time." Great poster, lousy movie. 1960.

Ghost of Dragstrip Hollow: This full-sheet poster for a B movie is more comic than dramatic, with a runaway T-bucket filled with seven crazy kids. 1959.

Hot Rod Gang: A section of the One-Sheet poster shows the great art detailing that makes this *Hot Rod Gang* movie image so enjoyable. 1958.

The Giant Gila Monster: This 1959 monster/hot rod horror flick is laughable but its great music and hot rods make it enjoyable. This lobby card is one of a large set of cards for the movie. 1959.

The Spider: "Will Eat You Alive!" Ed Kemmer, June Kenny, and Gene Persson fought off the spider which "Nothing . . . Can Stop!" This stunning lobby card with its nostalgia-style, half-fendered roadster is a classic and well worth the search to find. 1958.

The Wild Ride: This lobby card shows an early Jack Nicholson film about a murdering hot rodder with plenty of action, drinking and driving, and running from the cops via a Roadster pickup and a 1958 Chevy. 1960.

Bikini Beach: "See the beach party gang go dragstrip." Frankie Avalon and Annette Funicello at their best, with Annette in a polka-dot two-piece lusting after Frankie while dragsters run three abreast. A memorable three-sheet poster. 1964.

Hot Rod Hullabaloo: "Speed's their creed!" according to the headline on this one-sheet poster. It was the jet-age crowd who came to the hot rod hullabaloo. Hot rods, stock cars, and Formula 1 cars tear across the paper. 1966.

The Choppers: This low-buck lobby card for this lower-buck movie about teens, car thieves, hot rods, and cops, speaks of "fuel injected action!" An interesting selection of posters and lobby cards available. 1961.

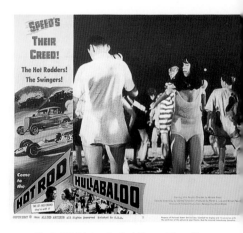

Hot Rod Hullabaloo: On the lobby card "speed" was still "their creed" for the hot rodders and the swingers. A movie with a sizable lobby card selection. 1966.

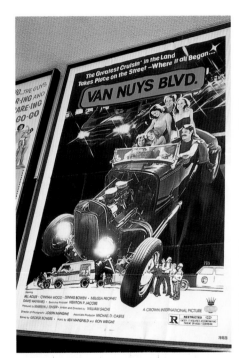

Van Nuys Blvd.: This movie is set in Southern California in the 1970s and follows the same old formula: love, lust, cops, and hot rods, plus a great poster. 1979.

Out Of Sight: This hot rod/rock and roll spy-spoof movie poster mixed an image of the Barris-built twin-engined ZZR hot rod with photos of six rock groups. Not a must, but collectible. 1966.

American Graffiti: A great memorable movie with nifty full-color lobby cards featuring Milner's 1932 five-window coupe. The script for the movie is also highly collectible and can be found in Hollywood. 1973.

In hot rodding's primeval years, small companies began to offer a diverse selection of speed parts. These companies started out in all sorts of small locations and primitive settings. For example, Dean Moon started his business in a one-stall garage in his backyard, and Vic Edelbrock began in a small gas station.

At the outset, these performance pioneers built parts for speedway and dry lakes racing, and because of their advertising, a collector of hot rod history can grasp the uniqueness of this sport and the people who made it flower into an international pastime.

A great advantage of collecting these ad images is that they take up little space. Most collectors use high-quality laser copies stored in photo album pages; storing them this way allows the ads to be looked over and enjoyed like a regular book while preserving the originals.

Ads from the 1940s and early 1950s are simple and interesting. They recall the folks who not only made hot rod hardware but built the cars and set the trends. The hot rod parts these companies advertised were limited but included heads, cams, manifolds, headers, and ignitions, and the accumulation of these early ads informs the collector as to when the companies emerged, what were popular products, and how primitive the parts were.

Ads were placed by custom builders and custom shops for many kinds of items and services. They appeared in *Hot Rod*, *Honk*, *Road & Track*, *Motor Trend*, *Throttle*, *Speed Age*, and *Speed Mechanics*.

Among the custom builders, the Barris brothers on Compton Avenue in Los Angeles, were the first to start advertising their unique services. It is interesting to note that in his 1949 ad George Barris had not yet begun to use his signature "K" for Kustom. The Barris shop provided body streamlining, channeling, top-chopping, custom painting services, and installation of push-button doors. Other shops involved in custom work also advertised but only on a small scale and with tiny ads. Glen Houser, owner of the Carson Top Shop on Vermont Avenue in Los Angeles, offered his services for "Custom Built Padded Tops, Seat Covers and Roadster Upholstery."

Barris's Custom Shop on Compton Avenue in Los Angeles. 1949.

Not all performance parts were made in California. Elgin Machine Works Inc. built racing pistons in Elgin, Illinois. 1948.

Barris's Custom Shop on Compton Avenue in Los Angeles. 1949.

Roy Richter always had clean neat ads for Bell Auto Parts. 1948.

Speed equipment manufacturing had expanded enormously by the end of the 1940s. Vic Edelbrock placed quarter-page ads for his new 1949 catalog, offering "Racing and Power Equipment." When he moved from North Highland in Hollywood to West Jefferson in Los Angles, he renamed his business Edelbrock Equipment Company, and his full-page ads featuring the *So-Cal Speed Shop Special* record holder at Bonnevilles reflect this change.

During this time, many of the great performance companies were born and new technologies were developed. Harman & Collins in Los Angeles bannered their ad with "A Camshaft Alone never Broke a Record But . . ." with the meaning that an engine builder should use their cam to build his winning engine set-up. Eddie Meyer ads offered "Complete Equipment" for roadsters, midgets, race cars, and boats and featured his popular Speedway Dual Manifold.

Various companies followed the same route. One of them was the Weber Tool Company, which boasted Ak Miller's successful record at Bonneville in his needle-nosed modified roadster with a speed of 172 miles per hour. The ad also noted that Dawson Hadley's Class "C" Modified Coupe record was set at 160.134 miles per hour, using Weber F-4 Straightaway Grind cams.

Smith & Jones, another cam company, came on the scene offering Clay Smith Cams. Clay Smith became one of the most respected cam companies in the country and continues to operate today. Ed Iskenderian was an active advertiser and was ahead of the pack right from the start. His ads were artfully laid up with graphic style and really stood out.

Great names in flathead ignitions were Spalding and Kong. Thomas Spalding built converted ignitions for Fords and Chevrolets in Monrovia, California, while not so far away, in Glendale, Charles "Kong" Jackson custom, built ignitions for Fords and Mercurys and also offered a full line of Winfield cams. Kong Jackson still operates his small shop, maintaining a link with the beginning of the sport.

Barney Navarro at Navarro Racing Equipment, which is still operating today, offered special racing heads and manifolds in Glendale, California. His prices for racing heads for a Ford flathead V-8 were $72 to $74 and his manifolds started at $36.50. Some of Navarro's ads featured winning speedway roadsters of the time.

The Offenhauser Equipment Company, which also exists today, has a long and glorious past reaching from Indy to the dry lakes, Bonneville, and the street. In 1950, they were offering racing flathead heads for $70 and a complete line of speed equipment from other independent speed equipment manufacturers. Others in this same arena included Tattersfield-Baron, Evans Speed Equipment, and Chet Herbert.

Some speed shops were also manufacturers. Almquist Engineering & Mfg. in Milford, Pennsylvania, offered a line-up of their own products and a 25¢ catalog with "Speed Tips." Bell Auto Parts, owned by Roy Richter in Bell, California, also offered a line of speed parts.

The low cost of collecting ads is all part of the fun of hot rod collectibles. Laser copies allow collectors to assemble ads nondestructively and create a unique catalog of hot rod performance pioneers.

Top: More power for your "Stude" from Frank Morgan. Bottom: Air cooled oil filter, another nifty early accessory. 1948.

Chet Herbert had his own roller-tappet cam in Bonneville in 1951.

Right
By 1950 Ed Iskenderian was a major source of hot rod cams.

Weber Tool Company was a leader in cams by the end of the 1940s.

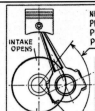
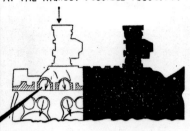
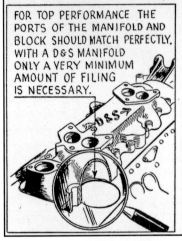

THAT NEW D&S MANIFOLD SURE PUTS THE SNAP INTO IT·· GIVES BETTER GAS MILEAGE TOO·· WOULD YOU LIKE TO SEE HOW IT WORKS?

THE CARBURETOR IS SET DIRECTLY OVER THE PORTS AND ALL PORTS ARE KEPT TO THE APPROXIMATE CAPACITY OF THE VALVE OPENINGS WHEN THE INTAKE VALVE IS WIDE OPEN. THIS GETS THE GAS AND AIR MIXTURE MOVING AT THE HIGHEST POSSIBLE VELOCITY.

NEARLY ALL OF THE PISTON TRAVEL TAKES PLACE IN THE SMALL PART OF THE STROKE.

INTAKE OPENS

INTAKE CLOSES

THE HIGH VELOCITY BUILT UP IN THE D&S MANIFOLD, CAUSES THE GAS & AIR MIXTURE TO CONTINUE TO FLOW AT A NEARLY EVEN RATE AT ALL DEGREES OF THE STROKE, WHICH HELPS PACK MORE GAS IN EACH CHARGE. THE HIGH VELOCITY NEVER ALLOWS RAW GAS TO SEPARATE FROM THE AIR AND SETTLE IN THE LOW POINTS OF THE MANIFOLD, TO LATER GO THRU THE MOTOR AS UNBURNED GAS. D&S MANIFOLD GUARANTEES BETTER GAS MILEAGE.

FOR TOP PERFORMANCE THE PORTS OF THE MANIFOLD AND BLOCK SHOULD MATCH PERFECTLY. WITH A D&S MANIFOLD ONLY A VERY MINIMUM AMOUNT OF FILING IS NECESSARY.

You'll get top performance with a D&S MANIFOLD

WRITE DIRECT OR SEE YOUR LOCAL DEALER FOR THE FOLLOWING CLARK HEADER CO. PRODUCTS LONG SHACKLES, HEADERS, CARBURETOR ADAPTORS, CHEVROLET HEADER & COMPLETE CHEVROLET DUAL SET EITHER WITH HEADER OR SPLIT MANIFOLD.

SEE YOUR LOCAL DEALER OR WRITE for free information

CLARK HEADER COMPANY

7049 E. FIRESTONE BLVD. DOWNEY, CALIFORNIA

Phone: TOpaz 27784

D & S Manifolds for flatheads gave "top performance." 1953.

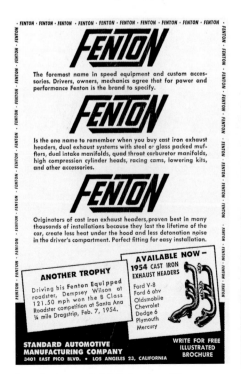

FENTON · FENTON · FENTON · FENTON · FENTON · FENTON · FENTON · FENTON · FENTON · FENTON

The foremost name in speed equipment and custom accessories. Drivers, owners, mechanics agree that for power and performance Fenton is the brand to specify.

Is the one name to remember when you buy cast iron exhaust headers, dual exhaust systems with steel or glass packed mufflers, dual intake manifolds, quad throat carburetor manifolds, high compression cylinder heads, racing cams, lowering kits, and other accessories.

Originators of cast iron exhaust headers, proven best in many thousands of installations because they last the lifetime of the car, create less heat under the hood and less detonation noise in the driver's compartment. Perfect fitting for easy installation.

ANOTHER TROPHY
Driving his Fenton Equipped roadster, Dempsey Wilson at 121.50 mph won the B Class Roadster competition at Santa Ana ¼ mile Dragstrip, Feb. 7, 1954.

AVAILABLE NOW –
1954 CAST IRON EXHAUST HEADERS
Ford V-8
Ford 6 ohv
Oldsmobile
Chevrolet
Dodge 6
Plymouth
Mercury

WRITE FOR FREE ILLUSTRATED BROCHURE

STANDARD AUTOMOTIVE MANUFACTURING COMPANY
3401 EAST PICO BLVD. • LOS ANGELES 23, CALIFORNIA

Fenton headers were built for both racing and the street. 1954.

FOR RECORD PERFORMANCE SELECT

Evans SPEED EQUIPMENT

boats · race cars · roadsters

HEADS & MANIFOLDS
FORD—MERCURY—STUDEBAKER

DUAL IGNITIONS
NITRO-ALKY CONVERSIONS

Custom Built Engines
Polished Crank Assemblies
Cams—Pistons
Chopped Flywheels
Fuel Blocks—Port & Relieve

The New Evans 4 Carb. Manifold $48.

2550 N. Seaman
El Monte, Calif.—FOrest 8-8286

Forty-eight dollars got you Evans' new "4 Carb. Manifold." 1950.

84

Eddie Meyer Hot Rod Parts fitted boats, race cars, midgets, and roadsters. 1949.

Kong Engineering was the name in high-speed ignitions. 1949.

In 1950 Douglass Muffler offered duals for a flathead Ford or Mercury.

Sharp S-P-E-E-D Equipment had an edge to it. 1950.

Harman & Collins ground the hot cams in 1949.

Edelbrock's new racing and power equipment catalog arrived in 1949.

Outstanding performance attained by the *So-Cal Speed Shop Special* with *Edelbrock Equipment.*

Class A two-way average, 156.39
Class C two-way average, 189.74
Class C fastest one-way, 193.54

Edelbrock Equipment Co.

4921 West Jefferson, Los Angeles 16, Calif., REpublic 29494

Screaming across the salt, Edelbrock parts provided "Outstanding" performance. 1950.

Glen Houser, the Carson Top inventor, ran small ads like this one in 1948.

Above and Left
Belond built racing headers for flatheads, while Smith and Jones turned out cams and custom engines. 1950.

~~130~~ 134.52 mph CHEVROLET

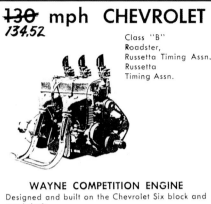

Class "B"
Roadster,
Russetta Timing Assn.
Russetta
Timing Assn.

WAYNE COMPETITION ENGINE
Designed and built on the Chevrolet Six block and crankshaft.
248 Cubic Inches—450 Pounds

WAYNE MFG. CO.
3205 FLETCHER DRIVE   LOS ANGELES 41, CALIF.
CL. 7-6352

Wayne Manufacturing, famous for their fast Chevrolets. 1950.

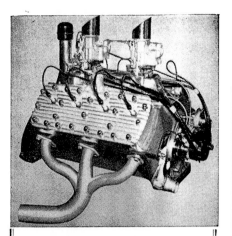

WEIAND
POWER & RACING EQUIPMENT

Increase Power, Speed & Economy with This Highly Polished Equipment on Your Ford or Mercury

Immediate Delivery at Your Dealers or

**2733 San Fernando Road
Los Angeles 65, California
Phone CApitol 0668**

Custom Engine Building
Now Being Done
FORD '60' - STUDEBAKER - MERCURY

Weiand, another great company for performance parts, which continues to flourish, had its roots in the post-war years. 1950.

SPALDING
CONVERTED IGNITIONS

Converted Ignition for Ford V-8, Ford 6, Mercury and Chevrolet
SEND FOR FREE FOLDER

Thomas P. Spalding
426 East Graystone Ave.   Monrovia, California
Phone Monrovia 162-71

Spalding ignitions were popular on the street and on the lakes at the end of the 1940s.

Navarro
Racing Equipment

HIGH COMPRESSION HEADS
DUAL MANIFOLDS
FOR
FORD V-8 AND MERCURY

NAVARRO RACING EQUIPMENT
718 S. Verdugo Rd., Glendale 5, Calif.

Navarro Racing Equipment, Barney at his best. 1950.

OFFENHAUSER

Ford-Mercury Heads, $70   V-8 "60" Heads, $66
Dual Manifold (reg.), $41   Dual Manifold '42-'47, $46
Plus 5% Federal Excise Tax and Express

 **◄ V-8 "60" HEAD**

CAMSHAFTS BY—
· Winfield
· Harman and Collins
· Weber
· Smith and Jones

A COMPLETE LINE OF SPEED EQUIPMENT

OFFENHAUSER Equipment Corp.
8936 National Blvd.   Los Angeles, Calif.

Offenhauser, famous from Indy to the dry lakes. 1950.

TATTERSFIELD-Baron
Scores Again

A new World's Record established by Wally Albright in "Haywire Kid" . . . 225 Class Cracker Box design . . . The fastest boat in its class.

ELECTRIC & CARBURETOR ENG. CO.
2323 E. 8th St.   Los Angeles, Calif.

Tattersfield-Baron scores again. 1950.

The advent of trading cards as a cheap method of promotion and advertising of sports teams and players has roots on both sides of the Atlantic. In England, the cards featured flowers, birds, airplanes, and automobiles and were put inside cigarette packets. America followed the trend with cards of sports teams, especially baseball. A hobby has grown from this beginning, which, today, commands the attention of hundreds of thousands of people who love to collect the cards.

Over the years, hot rod trading card sets have become very collectible. There has been a resurgence of hot rod cards recently. Among these are the set of Boyd Coddington's hot rod creations from Mothers Productions. Although we are listing only early collectible card sets, Coddington's 1994 set is worthy of inclusion in any hot rod card collection.

Cards of the 1960s did not have the uniformity of cards today. Three sizes were printed and issued: jumbo, postcard, and trading. There was even a trading card set that formed a jigsaw puzzle.

Two major card sets, offered from the early 1960s to the mid-1960s, were from two significant California hot rod and custom builders: George Barris and Ed Roth. Barris issued the earliest set. It was of a traditional trading card size and was sold in multiple packs of ten. The sets were divided into categories so that kids could collect the set and learn about hot rodding. They featured hot rods, dragsters, racers, and custom cars.

According to George Barris, "This allowed us to have a wide variety of cards which were hot rod related and it gave the series a framework instead of just a single mixed set." The hot rod and custom cards used photos that George had taken himself, while the racing photos came from other photographers.

The set features cards of many of the greatest hot rods and customs (or Kustoms as George prefers to call them) from the 1950s and the early 1960s. This first set contains the famous *Curley Flamed Ford*; Dave Cunningham's *Li'l Beauty* '40 Ford; the LeMans Cadillac; the *X-Tura* Thunderbird, Tom McMullen's flamed '32 drag racing roadster, *Li'l Coffin*, and Gene

Right
Barris released another set of regular trading cards of his movie cars, including the *ZZR* twin-engine hot rod and *Alvin's Acorn*. This card set was issued in the early 1970s.

This set of trading cards was produced by George Barris and features many of the vehicles he built over the years. They were classified as hot rods, custom cars, and dragsters.

This set of 4x6-inch trading postcards featured some of the great show and movie cars from the beginning of the 1960s: The *King-T*, *Surf Woody*, Carl Casper's *Telephone Booth* roadster, the *Munster Coach*, the Dobie Gillis *XMSC 210 Coupe*, and Roth's *Druid Princess*, and pink *Road Agent*.

Donruss marketed a set of cards that "displayed typical hot rods, dragsters, and Bonneville race cars a reader would see in *Hot Rod* magazine" as part of a 5¢ Hot Rod Bubble Gum candy pack.

Winfield's *Strip Star*. The back of each card gives their specifications and details. The sets were sold in green wrapped packs of 10, with graphics noting the contents. They were sold from a counter display box containing 100 packs.

Barris released several sets of cards until the beginning of the 1970s. His second major trading card set was redesigned and featured a new mix of cars. Many of them were the movie cars and hot rods he had built, including the *Mini Surfer* Mini Moke for the Beach Boys, the twin-engined *ZZR* hot rod for the movie *Out of Sight*, and the *Alvin Acorn*, a modified GTO used on the *Romp* TV show.

The reverse side of these nine cards created a jigsaw puzzle that formed a huge photo of George standing beside one of his comic show rods, the *Hard Hat Hauler*. During this time George also released a set of traditional postcards. On these he featured his great movie cars including the *Munster Coach*, *Drag-u-la*, *Ala Kart*, and the *Villa Riviera* Buick.

The second significant card set, from the model kit maker Revell, features Ed "Big Daddy" Roth's wild hot rods: *Outlaw*, the *Mysterion*, *Rotar*, and *Beatnik Bandit*. Other show rod postcards were of the *Car Craft Dream Rod*, built by Bill Cushenbery; Monogram's *Li'l Coffin*; and Joe Wilhelm's *Wild Dream*, a purple, narrowed T roadster. Most of this photography was done by Ron Freeman.

A hot rod trading card set was issued in 1964 by the Donruss Manufacturing Company in Memphis, Tennessee, in cooperation with *Hot Rod* magazine. Donruss marketed a set of cards which "displayed typical hot rods, dragsters, and Bonneville race cars that a reader would see in *Hot Rod* magazine" as part of a 5¢ *Hot Rod* Bubble Gum candy pack. The cards in this series also featured technical details and a short caption on the reverse side. They were wrapped with a flat slab of traditional pink bubble gum.

The hot rod cards are colorful, with slick photos of the hot rods, customs, and race cars that everyone loved in the 1960s. They can be stored in a folder or set in frames and displayed on the wall. Complete sets can be assembled which adds to the enjoyment of collecting them at trading card shows and hot rod swap meets.

It is difficult to price the cards. The biggest sector of trading card collecting is ball sports and some of these cards command enormous prices. Therefore the pricing of hot rod related cards pales by comparison. However, expect to pay at least $100 for an unopened set of mint cards. A counter display box, complete, easily sells for $500. Single cards run $8 through $20. Single unopened *Hot Rod* Bubble Gum packs run up to $60.

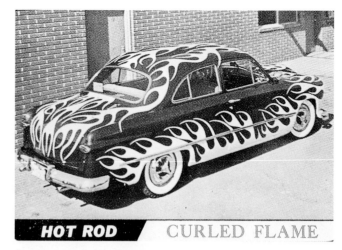

One of the cars in the hotrod series from George Barris featured Smiley's *Curley Flamed Ford*. 1960.

On the back of George Barris' latest trading card set, a nine card jigsaw puzzle could be assembled featuring George and the *Hard Hat Hauler*. 1972.

This pair of postcards featuring Cushenbery's *Matador* and Dave Stuckey's *Li'l Coffin* were sold at Larivee's International Championship Auto Shows. Mid-1960s.

Barris also produced larger versions of his regular trading cards for use as postcards. Most of these were sold on the International Championship Auto Shows circuit. Circa 1968.

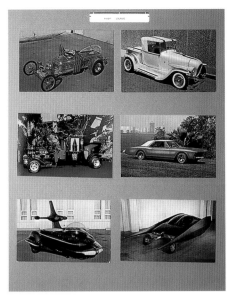

This set of postcard-size trading cards featured Roth's *Beatnik Bandit*, *Mysterion*, the *Outlaw*, and Joe Wilhelm's *Purple Wild Dream* roadster. Circa 1968.

Postcards also have their place in collectible cards. This panel of Barris-issued postcards features 6x4-inch cards of *Drag-u-la*, *Ala Kart*, *Munster Coach*, *Villa Riviera*, Roth's *Rotar*, and Bob Larivee's *Stiletto*. Circa 1968.

More of the Barris trading cards. The cars featured here include: Tom McMullens' '32 at the drags, *Li'l Coffin*, and Winfield's *Strip Star*. This set is the premium of all hot rod collectible cards.

Revell issued a series of Roth jumbo cards which were larger than postcards. *Beatnik Bandit*, circa 1964 shown.

Revell issued a series of Roth jumbo cards which were larger than postcards. *Outlaw*, circa 1964 shown.

Revell issued a series of Roth jumbo cards which were larger than postcards. *Rotar*, circa 1964 shown.

Another Roth card was this ripple-edged postcard of *Road Agent* that came from the old Harrah's Auto Museum in Reno, Nevada.

In recent years there has been a wide interest in collecting team clothing from professional ball teams and some of the prices paid for uniforms of top players are staggering. There is also a secondary stratum of clothing collecting that is auto related. Team items from Indy, NASCAR, and NHRA races encompassing racing suits, helmets, jackets, and shirts have become popular. Hot rod clothing was not considered collectible until recently but now the NSRA and Goodguys are mass merchandising hot rod clothing lines.

For the collector, the most valuable hot rod clothing collectibles are club jackets made in the 1950s and 1960s. These old jackets have created great interest and as there are so few pieces they command significant prices.

Style and look are first on a collector's list. A good-looking *Road Knights* jacket may not be as highly collectible as another club's jackets. *Road Knights* had up to 300 members while The *13 Gents* from Gardena, California, had only 13 members, and therefore only 13 jackets were stitched.

The club jacket concept took off after World War II when servicemen returned with their decorated leather "bomber" jackets. This was the image that the clubs in the 1940s and 1950s copied when they issued their own official club jackets. The jackets were distinctive depending on the location of the club, with brighter and jazzier jackets on the West Coast and more low key-styles on the East Coast.

It is important to note that club members treated their jackets as a badge of honor; the club commanded respect, and the owner respected the club's colors. Some older clubs still treat the ownership of their club jackets as an exclusive right. Some motorcycle clubs have this as a club bylaw, and a collector could find himself in physical danger if he

Right
George Barris checks out the program at the 1963 Portland Roadster Show while club members from around the state look on.

Cheaters club jacket from South San Francisco, made of wool with embroidered emblem, circa 1975.

Sports-Men club jacket from Southern California. Cotton and embroidery, circa 1955

Hop Up magazine created these collegiate jackets for staff members in 1951. Wool with leather sleeves.

Irwindale Raceway sold these jackets for promotion in the 1960s. Wool and embroidered letters.

The *Axle Busters* club jacket from San Jose, California, was more of a shirt than a jacket. It featured multi-colored embroidery, circa 1970.

The *Road Lords* from Whittier, California, created this cool collegiate-style purple, gold, and white letterman jacket with some fancy embroidery and a patch, circa 1958.

This club jacket for the *East Bay Aromas* is machine embroidered with a great cartoon of a blue eyed skunk driving a roadster. Wool collegiate style jacket with leather sleeves, circa 1958.

openly displayed such a jacket. Most car clubs are long defunct, so any ownership rights died with the last club meeting. It is only in recent years that these jackets have come onto the market at garage sales and swap meets.

The kind of jacket plays an important part in its collectibility. Simple cotton jackets with zippers and painted images like those of the *Riverside Knights Rods & Customs* are hand-painted and were a limited issue to members. The art was detailed, distinctive, and stylish on a red cotton background. Other light cotton jackets, like the *Axle Busters* of San Jose, were created with light embroidery and finely detailed in four colors. Like those of the *Riverside Knights*, the jacket's back panel image was cartooned and humorous.

Other clubs had more traditional and sophisticated jackets. Imitating what amounts to a high school letterman jacket, many 1950s and early 1960s clubs opted for the style of wool body, leather arms, and knitted cuffs.

The *East Bay Aromas* jacket is typical of this style, with a cartoon of a stinky skunk driving a '32 roadster. The lettering and image of the roadster and its skunk were heavily embroidered in beige, black, and light blue on a dark blue wool jacket with matching beige sleeves.

When *Hop Up* magazine went to Bonneville in 1953, they had their own jackets created for the trip. They were heavily embroidered with the image of a streamliner on the back. They also had extra embroidery on the chest with the magazine's name on one side and the jacket owner's name on the other side.

Other variations on these jackets include the *Half Moon Bay Drag Strip* sweater in black wool with a half zipper in the front and stylish red and white script embroidery on the back. *Irwindale Raceway* also created its own jacket with custom fuzzy lettering.

One of the all-time favorites is the *Swanx* customs club from Oakland, California. Their jacket featured a dark blue wool jacket with bright silver-white embroidery and a simple image of a custom Cadillac in the center. Another classic is the bright red wool *Road Kings Burbank* jacket with its gold crown and white Old English-style lettering.

Many of the best jackets were manufactured by DeLong, Rawlins, or Skookim and then custom embroidered by businesses like Stylized Emblem Company in Los Angeles, California, or any of the hundreds of small shops across the country.

Selecting and collecting jackets is a personal call and finding them is difficult; prices can be outrageous. Many jackets have been worn out, and the silk lining has decayed from body sweat, old age, or moths. Oil stains and general wear and tear devalue them instantly.

Storage is important once a jacket is purchased. Many club jackets are stored in a dark, cool, dry place, are moth-proofed and put in an airtight sealed suit bag.

Pricing is select and personal and may well run $100 to $500 for a good 1960s jacket. Even higher prices have been paid for pristine special-interest jackets.

Crank Busters club jacket is rare, from California. Heavily embroidered wool, circa 1960.

Chancellors club jacket from Van Nuys, California. Cotton, embroidery, and patch, circa 1970.

Cruisin Angels Car Club from Milwaukee, Wisconsin, used this black cotton and gold embroidered jacket, circa 1980.

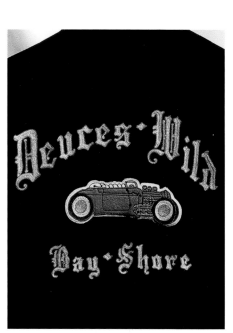

Deuces-Wild club jacket from the San Francisco bay area. Wool, embroidery, and patch, circa 1975.

Swanx of Oakland, California. A smart club jacket from a custom club. Wool and embroidery, circa 1965.

13 Gents from Gardena, California, a rare and unusual club jacket in wool and embroidery, late 1950s.

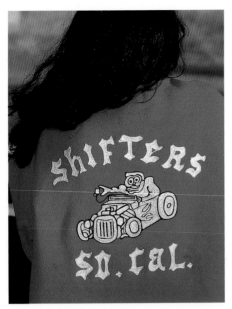

Shifters club jacket from Southern California, made of wool with embroidery, circa 1994.

Syndicate on Wheels Inc. from Sacramento, California, had a cotton jacket with multi-colored embroidery, circa 1970.

Half Moon Bay Drag Strip is one of hot rodding's cradles of creation. Embroidered wool sweater, very rare, circa 1958.

The *Hop Up* magazine jackets created for the Bonneville Nationals were superb and are extremely rare today. Wool body, leather arms, heavy embroidery.

Road Kings club jacket from Burbank, California. Wool, embroidery, and patch, circa 1968.

Riverside Knights was a small club and produced these hand-colored cotton jackets with a cartoon of a busty young lady riding a cam-rod, circa 1982.

16 CLUB PLAQUES

Club plaques have been issued since the 1930s. The first known plaque, in cast aluminum, was issued by the *Outriders,* which was formed in 1932. They are now considered to be the first hot rod club. The *Outriders* continue on today.

Before World War II, a few cast aluminum plaques were issued from dry lakes racing clubs and associations, and some, like the first *Road Runner* plaques, were hand-painted on cardboard. Other early plaques were hand-painted onto steel rectangles. A few clubs even created silk-screened plaques on flat sheet metal, like the *Rod Knockers* from Hollister, California.

Plaques were displayed on the rear bumper or in the back window, and by the 1950s, plaques had became a status symbol for hot rod and custom lovers. It signified that as a member of the club you had a reputation to uphold. The baddest clubs hung theirs on chains and dropped them from the center of the rear bumper so they flew in the breeze. It is claimed by some that because of this, pursuing police couldn't see the name that was inscribed on the plaque.

Club plaques offer the collector an enormous field for collecting. Not only did every town have at least one club, but over the years the club mutated or was replaced by another. If you multiply that by the number of good-sized towns in the state and the number of states in the nation, the quantity of plaques is amazing. The total number of different plaques that may have been produced in the past 50 years is probably somewhere around 20,000, but some collectors think that the number may be as high as 40,000. Sounds wild, but they are out there if you can find them.

Some collectors may focus on one state or county while others comb the West, the East, or the Midwest. Every area has plenty of material to look for, but like the club jackets, only limited quantities of some plaques exist. Numbers as small as 10 are not unusual and 100 would be a large casting.

In the 1950s, club members were far more inventive than folks today in the making of these plaques. They created a design, and then went to a pattern maker who carved the reversed design in wood. Using this wooden pattern, the club members would then cast their own plaques, having learned the casting technique in machine shop while in high school. The majority of clubs took their patterns to a foundry where impressions of the pattern were made in casting sand. Hot liquid aluminum was poured into the sand mold and the plaque was cooled into a rough casting.

It was cleaned of slag and ground along the edges, and at this point, it was either picked up by the club and refinished by its members, or finished by the foundry with polish and paint. These were the days before the Environmental Protection Agency got on our tails about air pollution; many of these small foundry operations were later forced to close.

This rare and unusual silk-screened club plaque is from the *Rod Knockers* from Hollister, California, circa 1950.

Hot rod and custom clubs had their own plaques, and new sizes and shapes appeared made out of bronze, brass, and aluminum, circa 1970.

In the post-war years, hot rod clubs flourished and each club had to have a plaque of its own. These are all from around the Los Angeles area, circa 1946.

All the early SCTA-affiliated dry lakes clubs had their own plaques, circa 1946.

There were several foundries famous for their casting of plaques: Koehler Foundry in Bell, California; Chicago Metal, which had foundries in at least three locations around the nation; Stylized Emblem Company in Hollywood, California; and Speed Gems on the East Coast. Most of the foundries stamped their work; Koehler Foundry used a 1-inch sided triangle with their name and a large K in the center.

The plaques displayed here are from hot rod and custom clubs. Most of the plaques matched the size of the state license plates. The plaque and the license plate could be arranged symmetrically at the rear of the car.

A second style was for the club's name to sit boldly above the rectangle. This added a little more flair to the plaque. Examples of this style are the plaques from the *Sir Guys of Torrance* or the *Argauns of Downey*.

A third style was to create a shield that fitted into the space of the regular rectangle plaque. The *Tisians* and the *Pharaohs*, both of Southern California, used this style.

A fourth, more artistic style, created some of the most interesting plaques of all. The plaque was sculpted, and the club's name was then cast into that design. The *Auto Butchers of East Los Angeles* featured a small butcher's cleaver in black with the club name polished out in aluminum, while the *4 "Barrel"* club plaque

features four beer barrels in black with a large red 4 on the front barrel. These plaque were simple and graphic, and said it all—this club had fast rods and a good time. The *Twisters* from Alta Vista also had a neat variation—a twisty plaque, which suited their name.

A variety of finishes were applied. The basic most simple plaques were simple polished aluminum lettering on a black background. Others used background colors from baby blue to maroon and red. Some were cast in bronze, then polished gold and painted with a colored background. The very rare Barris-issued *Kustom's Los Angeles* plaques were created this way.

Not all plaques were issued by clubs: *Lone Wolf*, *Night Prowler*, and *No Club*, among others, were for individuals who wanted to be a nonclub member. Many of these were J.C. Whitney products and some custom plaques can still be ordered from their catalog.

Pricing of plaques varies in different parts of the country. There are many reproductions now being circulated and these are extremely difficult to tell from originals. In fact, a joke among collectors is that the way to tell an original from a reproduction is by its price, the original is cheaper! Originals range from $20 to $100, and reproductions sell for $20 to $40.

As the years went on, the design became more intricate and adventurous, like the *Squires* and the *Monarchs* plaques, circa 1960.

The greater majority of plaques were polished aluminum with black backgrounds; some added a little color as highlights, circa 1958.

This set of Southern California plaques displays some very nice graphics and fine casting, especially with the Torrance *Sir Guys*, circa 1968.

Kustom's Los Angeles, organized by George Barris, soon expanded into the *Kustoms of America*. The *Auto Butchers* of East Los Angeles had one of the neatest plaques of all time, with a meat cleaver as their plaque.

Four dry lakes racing clubs, circa 1950.

Clubs as far afield as Hawaii had plaques, including the *Beachcombers*, circa 1962.

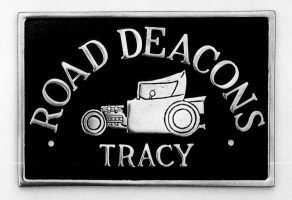

The *Riverside Rickshaws* and the *Road Deacons* from Tracy, the *Turtles* from Filmore, and the *Rail Hustlers* from La Canada, California, had different sized and shaped plaques as this panel shows, circa 1958.

Plaques became even more detailed and comic towards the end of the 1960s, including the *Crack Ups* and the *Side Winders* from San Berdoo, circa 1959.

Above Left
Some plaques were not from clubs. *The Lone Wolf* and the *Outlaws* came from J.C. Whitney's catalog, circa 1962.

Left
The *Coachmen*, the *Gatorettes*, the *Challengers*, and the *Madaladins* set their own style in the late 1950s.

Top

The variety of club names is amazing: the *Cut-Outs*, *Choppers*, *Road Saints*, and *Argauns* are just some of the club names that were seen, circa 1957.

Middle

The *Knights* seem to have a handle on the club scene.

Bottom

These four plaques are classics, especially the *Stackers*, the *Studs*, and *R.P.M. Boys*, circa 1956.

The Koehler Foundry in Bell, California, was famous for its plaques and stamped the castings with their triangular crest.

There were more knights than you could believe: the *Roadknights*, *Road Knights*, and the *Sinister Knights*, to name a few, circa 1960.

Right

If you weren't a *Knight* you might have been a *Devil*, or you could have been an *Angel*, but you might have been a *Jugger*, circa 1960.

Four early California club plaques made of cast aluminum, polished and painted, circa 1955.

Each of these four plaques has an unusual twist, circa 1955.

There have been so many clubs in the Los Angeles area in the past 50 years that the number of plaques may amount to 1,000 or more. These four are from the 1950s.

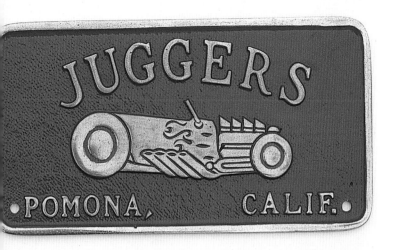

These four classic plaques were roughly cast, polished, and painted in the traditional manner, circa 1958.

The artwork on these plaques is simplistic but the detail they show carries the message clearly, circa 1960.

The *Creators*, the *Dools*, *Road Gents*, and the *Tisians* were Los Angeles clubs who cast their mark with their own stylish plaques.

Restored club plaques make a great display when polished and painted, circa 1962.

DECALS

The first hot rod decals I owned were a pair of 4-inch high-water transfer Mooneyes. I considered them my initial "performance equipment" purchase. I was sure they made my father's Falcon go 15 miles per hour faster. Having the Moon decal on your rod was like getting a tattoo, it pronounced your car as bad, and even today, many primered rods and customs have Mooneyes glued to their quarter panels, or have smaller versions stuck in the corners of their side windows.

Water transfer decals came about in the 1920s. They were used by many kinds of manufacturing industries to signify their products, specifications, or user directions. They were stuck on electric motors, airplane parts, auto parts, and toys. Then they began appearing on automobile windows from tourist destinations and dealers.

Travel destination decals started out as stick-on steamer trunk labels which were made out of paper. These labels endured, their colors were bright, and they were practically waterproof once they dried. After World War II, vacation decals could be bought in every nickel-and-dime store in every town in the country.

The transfers were manufactured by offset litho-printing, and later by silk screening, onto a clear ultra-thin flexible plastic base. Hundreds could be printed on a single sheet, making mass production simple and cheap.

Speed equipment manufacturers saw this as a great opportunity to obtain free advertising, especially if the decals were on a great-looking, fast-running, car. Edelbrock, Isky, and Moon, as well as Speed Specialties, had their own decals.

One of the most popular was the Custom Cams decal from Speed Specialties in Pacific Palisades, California. It featured a voluptuous lady in a flowing red dress riding on a cam shaft. If you were game to run this decal on your rod you got an extra 10 hero points.

Hot Rod magazine offered transfer decals featuring Tom Medley's *Stroker* cartoon character while others featured just the *Hot Rod* magazine logo. At first these were only given to people whose machines

Right
Water-and self-adhesive decals are part of the hot rod collectible offerings. Everyone, from Ed Roth to Isky to Moon and Hurst have issued decals.

The Cash Auto water slide decals featured all the right racing parts along with a Lucky 7 on the helmet. Cash Auto was a San Francisco Speed Shop. Circa 1958.

This early water slide decal for Offenhauser in the early 1950s offers the Perfect Combination.

Carrell Speedway offered this Jalopy Races window water slide decal to patrons in the early 1950s.

appeared in the magazine and they became a status symbol, a kind of "Hot Rodding Seal of Approval." Later on, *Car Craft* and *Rod & Custom* also issued their own magazine decals.

For quite a while in the 1950s, it was considered very cool to have decals on the back window from half a dozen of the best high performance companies. Maybe they didn't make the car go faster, but they inferred there was "hot stuff" under the hood. Small detail decals became popular in the shape of bullet holes, spiderweb lacing, and little flower chains to decorate the car windows.

Standard company logos like Howard Cams' red, white, and blue logo with a large red cog as the background, was typical of the time. Similarly, Schiefer Manufacturing's logo featured a gold cog with a red arrowhead.

Another idea used cartoons as decals. Ansen, in Los Angeles, turned out a number of them, including the Posi-Shift with a red roadster screaming off the line, pistons and rods whizzing, while Iskenderian Racing Cams had their clown cartoon, and Offenhauser portrayed a hot rod tortoise.

Moon followed the trend with his Mooneyes, offering left and right facing eyes in five sizes, along with his "Cool Eyes" and cartoon of the Mooneyes dragster. Today, Mooneyes still sells these traditional water slide decals in sheets with left and right Mooneyes, a Cool Eyes and a round yellow Moon.

Most of the single decals came in one size of about 4 inches square. Many companies gave retailers large decals from 6 inches to around 15 inches to display in shop windows and on their glass counters.

Water transfer decals lost their popularity in the 1970s and were replaced by self-sticking decals.

The classic sheet of Mooneyes decals is still available after all these years. Left- and right-facing eyes in several sizes are on the sheet.

These had an image silk screened onto a colored vinyl plastic film with a peel-off back.

There was a more serious side to these decals. Drag racers, road racers, and boat racers displayed corporate decals to show sponsor support and product endorsement. Today, these decals are mandatory on race cars. Sponsors want their names to be seen, and in some types of racing, placing the right decals on the cars pays money. Every one of those decals stuck on a NASCAR vehicle indicates corporate sponsorship.

Collecting decals is fun and relatively inexpensive. Many 1960s decals are still around and can be obtained from the original company. Others are to be found at swap meets and from dealers including Thompson's Auto Literature which sells quite a large selection at West Coast swap meets. Many companies still give away free decals at races and with catalogs. The majority of these new decals are self-adhesive vinyl.

Pricing of decals found at swap meets and shows runs from $1 to $30. Some big-scale store window decals, such as the huge Dougs Headers' decals, featuring an orange 1940 Willys, can run as high as $100. However, average prices for small window decals are generally around $5.

Moon Automotive's first decal featured a T-roadster in red or green. This water slide decal is from about 1955.

This original Speed Specialties, Custom SS Cams decal is one of the most famous, and still one of the most popular window decals of all time. Once again sex sells. Circa 1952.

In the 30 years since this decal was issued, the Deist company evolved from a drag chute manufacturer to one of the nation's premier racing safety equipment manufacturers. Getz offered racing gear ratios to track and street racers alike. Both these water slide decals are rare, circa 1960.

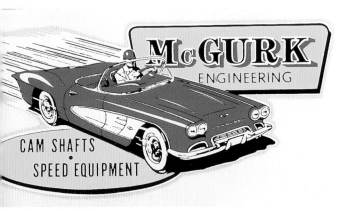

This McGurk Engineering water slide decal features a gorgeous graphic of a racing Corvette. Circa 1959.

Many water slide decals were made to sit in the rear window like these two five-inch beauties from Grant Piston rings and Weber Tool Company. Circa 1960.

These two water slide decals are rare and highly collectible and are from two famous performance companies, Schaller and Schiefer. Schaller's 1/4 Speed Cam was a trick performance item which failed to make any impact on racing, and Schiefer made the best drag racing flywheels and clutches. Circa 1960.

PRECISION ENGINEERED **Offenhauser** EQUIPMENT

This trio of water slide decals are from some of California's hottest hot rod parts manufacturers. Moon and Offenhauser still exist, while Hildebrandt is remembered for inlet manifolds and valve covers. Circa 1954.

Steen's skunk decal smells as sweet as a rose. These cute skunk cartoon decals for racing lubricants from the 1960s are rare, as are the Tony Nancy self-adhesive decals from the mid-1980s.

Howard Cams and Ansen added to the mass of hot rod decals that appeared in the late 1950s and early 1960s. Ansen's "Posi-Shift" looked like it could get out of control very easily!

PINS, BADGES, 18 AND DASH PLAQUES

Collecting hot rod related pins and badges parallels collecting military medals and decorations. It can be just as colorful and interesting, especially when you discover that there is a huge diversity of pins, dash plaques, and badges available.

A hot rod pin, a dash plaque, or badge is produced every time there is a hot rod event. They were issued at rod runs, picnics, races, Bonneville, the dry lakes, and many hot rod shows and promotions. Sometimes all three are available, and very frequently, ID badges worn by officials are also available.

The wearing of pins started in the old days when officials wore a badge of office for every kind of event. The badges signified their participation in the event and the importance of the wearer. Collectors gather promotional badges from drag racing events, auto manufacturers, professional organizations, tire makers, and even taxi companies and insurance companies.

The diversity of pins and badges is enormous. Every section of the country and every state has its own offering of hot rod collectibles. National events also turn out numerous collectibles. Over the years, these items have ranged from traditional pinback badges made of paper, celluloid or acetate plastic, or metal, to embroidered cloth badges, and silk-screened dash plaques and hat pins.

The badges for hot rodding reach back to the days of early dry lakes racing and official identification badges. Dash plaques were awarded by the Russetta Timing Association and the SCTA. These are covered in the Hot Rod Awards chapter as they are an award of merit for a record speed, rather than a simple "I was there" plaque.

Embroidered cloth badges promoting a company were originally made for drivers and teams to attach to their racing suits, but they were soon produced for sale to the public. Bonneville and the dry lakes created their own embroidered cloth badges as did high performance companies like Isky, Moon, Edelbrock, and Hurst.

Many of these items are still available as their traditional use for decorating race clothing continues.

At one time, collecting cloth badges was a national craze. Today they still hold the collectors' interest, just like decals. All the major high performance companies offered embroidered cloth badges at some time, including Moon, Edelbrock, Ansen, Weiand, and Isky.

This ultra rare "Think Pink" pinback badge is from Ed Pink Racing Engines and was handed out at drag races to remind racers that Pink was the guy who should build their next engine. 3 inches, 1966.

This gold-thread embroidered jacket patch from the American Auto Racing Writers & Broadcasters Association was owned by Dean Moon. He was a member of this professional organization for many years and wore the patch as a badge of honor.

Dean Moon helped sponsor many events and at the second Slowpokes Annual Rod Run, his Mooneyes appeared on the participant's pinback badge. 3 inches, circa 1968.

This set of rare Bonneville badges belonged to Dean Moon. They are highly collectible as they were limited to those who attended the event. 2 inches.

Hot Rod magazine had a 10th anniversary Fishing Party to Catalina Island and took along a mass of advertisers for the event. Hot Rod magazine cartoonist Tom Medley created a roadster-boat named The Thing just for the badge. 1959.

A collector could begin his search with a visit to a large swap meet. Dealers can often be found selling several hundred assorted embroidered badges. Collectors generally display these items in folders with the patches attached to the pages by a light adhesive.

Another sought-after item is pinback badges. Bonneville, or "B/Ville," has used a pinback for participants, spectators, the press, and officials for many years. They are great collectibles. The earlier the year, the harder they are to find, and the more expensive they are. Pinbacks were used by many organizations for three good reasons: They were impossible to duplicate easily at short notice without a machine, they were cheap to make, and they were hard to lose once attached.

The most popular collectible pins are those commemorating contemporary hot rod runs, and these are divided into two groups. The hat pins and dash plaques from these runs are proving to be incredibly popular. Virtually every major rod run from the past ten years has produced its own hat pin or dash plaque, and many of the runs have produced both.

Dash plaques have always been designed to do just what the name implies, namely, be put on the dash. At first these were fine for their intended use, but as the popularity of hot rodding events grew, the number of plaques increased. Suddenly, the dash could no longer accommodate all the plaques given out in one season.

Folks attending these events no longer put the item on their vehicles. Instead they put them away or created a collection. Events like the Rod Powell Picnic in Monterey, California, has produced dash plaques from each annual event for many years. At one time, major events, such as the Oakland Roadster Show, also created their own cast aluminum dash plaques for participants. Today these are considered some of the most valuable and interesting plaques of all.

The production of hot rod hat pins has exploded like mice breeding in a barn. At some time, every hot rod shop, custom builder, custom paint shop, organization, magazine, manufacturer, and major event has had a hat pin or two. These small items, designed to go on a hat with a pin and clasp, signify either the owner's participation in the event or satisfaction with an item.

There are generic hat pins, too. Some are comical, noting for example, "Anyone can restore a car but it takes real man to chop one," while others feature a dropped axle, a Ford logo, a custom car, or a Carson Top style.

Collectors use two main methods of display for pinbacks; they page them in the manner of cloth badges or baseball cards, or for a more open display, attach them to a piece of fabric like a curtain or a wall hanging.

Collecting these items is relatively cheap. Pinbacks from the 1960s run from $5 to $25 with rare pins going for as much as $50. Embroidered patches go from $2 to $20 depending upon size and detailing, although some highly detailed dress patches can price as high as $50. Event hat pins run from $1 to $8, with rare items somewhat higher.

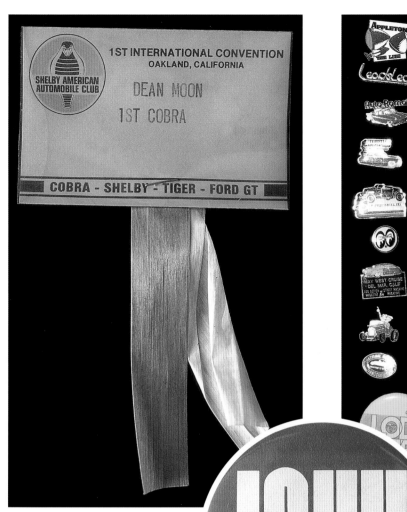

This paper, ribbon, and plastic ID tag belonged to Dean Moon. He was honored at the 1st International Convention of the Shelby Automobile Club in Oakland, California, as part of the team that created the first Cobra.

It would seem that every company in hot rodding, and every event, has a hat pin, so collecting them is easy, cheap, and fun. Like dash plaques, there are tens of thousands of different hat pins out there. Displaying them on hats or curtains seems to be best way to show the collection.

Isky could have made a believer out of you with his pinback badge in 1974. 3 inches.

This rare Member patch is from the Bonneville Nationals in 1974. 3 inches, embroidered cotton patch.

The Press has always had Press Passes, and this one from 1971 was issued to Dean Moon, who photographed the event for several magazines. 3 inches.

Dash plaques have become a rash on the dash. Once held in high esteem, today most are dispatched to the fridge door, the bottom drawer, or the garage wall. This selection is from Rod Powell's collection.

AWARDS

Collecting awards, plaques, and trophies can be compared to collecting gold records. The collector had nothing to do with the record, but it represents a victory or turning point in someone's life or career. Folks who have an interest in these items like to focus on who was presented with the award, while others are only interested in the variety and artistic style of the objects.

Luckily there is a vast field of items to choose from. Hundreds of thousands of these pieces have been issued from every race, organization, and event ever held for hot rodding. Initially, these awards came from racing organizations and later from clubs. The awards were given for the new race records or for the first three places.

The early hot rod shows held at Urich-Gibb Mercury in Whittier, California, gave wall plaques and dash plaques to participants. These early shows, organized by Dean Moon and the *Hutters Car Club*, were part of the grassroots movement of hot rodding.

Items from these shows can still be found, but at a premium price.

Hot rod award collecting includes race trophies along with wall and dash plaques from hot rod and custom shows, the dry lakes, Bonneville, and the drag races. They can be found at garage sales, swap meets, antique shops, and through personal contact with award winners.

In the 1950s and 1960s, show awards grew to enormous sizes. A first-place winner at a major car show might get a 4-foot or even a 6-foot-high trophy to take home and display. Gene Winfield recalls filling an entire garage with trophies. Eventually he needed the space and his solution was to keep all the plaques and trophy heads and trash the trophies, hauling a full pickup truck load to the city dump. This story not only illustrates the problem of keeping the trophies because of their size but points out why they are so rare today.

This certificate of appreciation from the Larsen/Cummins LSR team was presented to people who contributed to the Class "D" streamliners' successful Bonneville record attempt in 1967.

The National Hot Rod Association used to present a Certificate of Performance when a national class record was broken. This certificate from 1963 was for an A Modified/Sports class win by *Moonbeam*, the Chevy-powered Devin owned by Dean Moon.

This rare cast metal plaque from the 1953 Motorama Show was given to exhibitors and show entrants as awards.

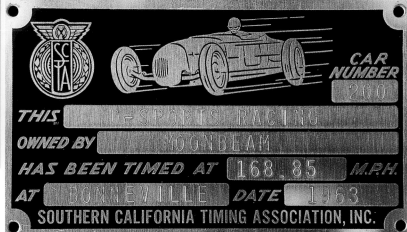

Like Gene Winfield's sensible solution, collecting just the plaques or the trophy heads is now common among collectors. Some of the trophies are well worth collecting for their art. They are only 12 inches high and are made of polished hardwood with engraved plaques, topped with great little hot rod sculptures.

Collecting trophy heads, especially from the early 1950s, is somewhat like collecting miniatures of today's highly expensive collectors' editions of hot rod sculptures. These trophy heads range from primitive to refined art, and some are delightfully detailed.

Dashingly styled roadsters were mounted on early Bonneville and dry lakes awards. There are about four variations of roadsters from that time. These little hot rod sculptures represented the exciting action of dry lakes racing and no doubt helped to spawn the modern hot rod bronzes we are offered today for thousands of dollars.

With the rapid expansion of hot rod and custom shows in the early 1950s, trophy heads started appearing for hot rods other than roadsters. By the mid-1950s, a selection of other trophy heads appeared, including several track-nosed three-window '32 Ford coupes, a chopped three-window '32 Ford, a custom '37 Ford, and several custom '40 Fords. In the late 1950s there was a mass of these little sculptures. A variety of customs appeared, including Mercurys, Dodges, and Chevrolets, reflecting the changing interest of the show participants and the diversity of shows.

Trophy head collectors have taken to displaying their collections by putting them on a base of either marble or hardwood, like a miniature display sculpture. This makes mounting and exhibiting simple.

The 1960s saw a change in trophy ideas. During this time another style of award became popular: wall plaques. There are several different types of wall plaques: paper awards, which had to be framed; cast bronze and aluminum plaques, which were generally engraved; and photo-etched gold or silver plaques, which used hand-engraved personalizing and a wooden mount.

These wall plaques were awarded not only by car clubs but by show promoters, equipment manufacturers, and show organizations. For example, the fledgling International Show Car Association gave out plaques for either winning an event or for services to the organization.

Another award collecting area is dash plaques from Bonneville and the dry lakes. These were awarded by rival timing associations, the Russetta Timing Association and the SCTA. Today, many of these items are still revered by their winners, but every so often a collection is offered or a single item is traded.

Prices vary widely for these items. Trophy heads command $5 to $25; complete trophies' prices are dependent upon who the recipient was, how famous the award is, and how badly it is wanted. The price can run from $10 to $200. Wall plaques are similarly priced. Old Russetta and SCTA timing plaque prices are not known, but expect to pay a premium for such unique items.

The National Hot Rod Association used to have an annual Hot Rod and Custom Show combined with the Winternationals in Pomona. This Award for Excellence from the 1962 show is made of a photo-printed gold anodized plate and a wood base.

This Award for Excellence from the 1964 Winternationals Custom Auto Fair is highly collectible. Collectors create great wall displays with this kind of item.

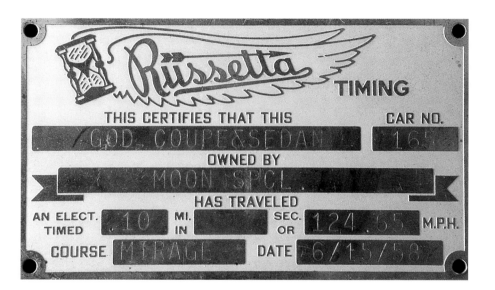

These small brass plates were designed to serve double duty: first as a dash plaque, secondly, and more importantly, as an award of merit for setting a new record or breaking an existing one. They could be fixed to the dash of a car to show how fast the car had run. This Russetta Timing plaque certified that the *Moon Special* had run 124.65 miles per hour at EL Mirage on June 15, 1958.

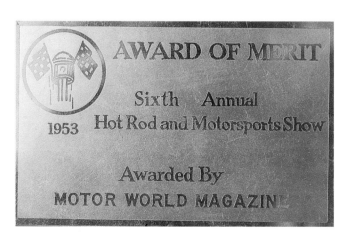

Some of the rarest awards are from the earliest hot rod shows. This Award of Merit was presented in 1953 by *Motor World Magazine*.

This presentation plaque from the first Hot Rod Show at Urich and Gibb Motor Company in Whittier, California, in 1950 is extremely rare. It was one of the first hot rod shows around in the early 1950s.

Small clubs such as the Hutters awarded members annual trophies for consistent wins like this one to the Moon Brothers for their dry lakes racing.

Instead of dash plaques, the Strokers awarded trophies for class records at the dry lakes in 1948.

Some awards were traditional trophies, like this one from the second hot rod show at Urich/Gibb, the Lincoln/Mercury dealer in Whittier, California.

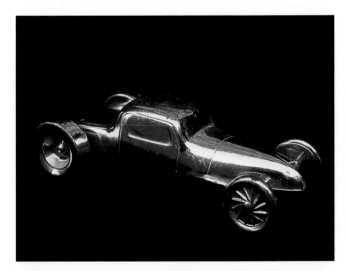

Many kinds of trophy heads have been created over the years including roadsters, coupes, and streamliners. This gorgeous '32 roadster originally graced a dry lakes award.

This gold-plated streamlined coupe trophy head looks like a Bonneville award, but more than likely it was used on a hot rod club award from the 1960s.

A large variety of items are available to collect, or to add to collections, that don't fit into the common categories. These include posters, packaging, accessories, and T-shirts. Collecting them can be a lot of fun as many are not as sought after as mainstream hot rod collectibles.

Some of these items are not hot rod related but use the hot rod title freely to indicate an "outlaw" image. The "Hot Rod Bicycle Accessory" is typical of these items. This unit was a sound-maker that could be attached to the back wheel of a child's bicycle. It made the sound of a motor running as the bike was pedaled and was made from an aluminum tube painted to look like an exhaust pipe tip. It was sold by the Hot Rod Company on West 7th Street in Los Angeles.

Some collectors have focused on one brand name only for the past 50 years. A prime example is

the Moon Equipment Company in Santa Fe Springs, California. Many collectors specialize in the many colorful and diverse items made by Moon through the years. Their products have encompassed just about every collectible, from signature wheel discs, and signature products including T-shirts and regular shirts, to catalogs, racing parts, hat pins, news releases, and model kits. They also put out decals, Moon shoes, and gas tanks with Moon logos.

The owners of the Moon Company have long been aware of the positive response the Mooneyes logo receives. The huge variety of Moon stuff is all the more interesting because the company has been around since the beginning of the 1950s and its mass of collectibles continues today with an even wider selection.

Racing and high performance parts also offer a wide variety of collectible packaging from manufacturers

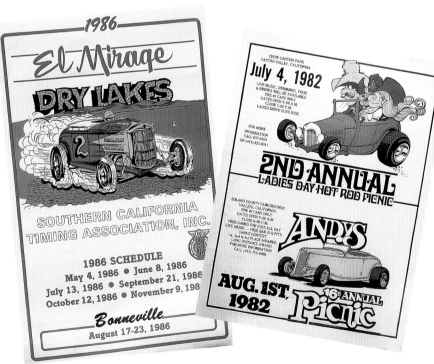

This El Mirage Dry Lakes poster noted all the dates for events. 1986 edition, approximately 20 inches.

This flyer poster printed in four colors advertised two Brizio hot rod events in 1982. 11 inches.

There were thousands of show posters printed over the years. This one from the Santa Rosa Auto Show features George Barris *Ala Kart* dream truck. It was printed on card stock in two colors. 24 inches, circa 1963.

Other free-form artworks, like this wall panel of a custom Buick, are neat to collect. Expect to pay top dollar, as these are one-off original works of art. Artist, Von Franco.

such as Edelbrock, Weiand, and Isky Racing Cams. The boxes in which cams, bearings, wheels, rockers, and carburetors were shipped in sometimes featured interesting box art that can be added easily and cheaply to any collection.

Some folks collect racing hardware—heads, inlet manifolds, exhaust headers, and accessories. High performance engine parts are also highly collectible. However, since they are often re-used in nostalgic hot rods and customs, they are not covered in this book. Racing parts that are no longer legal or useful have high collectibility. Small Moon gas tanks, hand pressure pumps, and supercharger cases can make interesting shelf art.

Posters from old hot rod related events are another popular kind of paper collecting. Many collectors have wide tastes for this art mixing together, for example, Joie Chitwood's Daredevils in their 1950 Fords along with posters from movies and the old hot rod shows.

Old hot rod show posters have become very collectible. Many of the early posters were printed on poster board and have survived much better than later illustrations printed on paper. It is interesting to note that these shows were not often advertised as hot rod shows but rather as auto shows. An example is the Santa Rosa, California, Auto Show in 1960 which featured George Barris's famous Oakland Roadster Show winner *Ala Kart*.

Other posters that are highly prized are from Bonneville and the Southern California dry lakes. Early editions are rare and quite valuable, and some, like the 1963 Bonneville poster, are being reproduced. The dry lakes racers have a long line of posters that have been produced over the years. Traditional hot rod events like Andy's Picnic, Fathers' Day, and the Goodguys events have all created posters over the years. These are quite rare and worth collecting for framed displays in dens and garages.

Collectible clothing items may use images of hot rod memorabilia and include T-shirts, shorts, and even shoes. Goodguys has offered a line of flamed shorts, shirts and shoes for the last few years and no doubt in the future these will be highly prized, as old Moon shirts and shoes are today.

T-shirts have been part of the hot rod scene since its inception, and finding original items is extremely rare. All the old hot rod shops, hot rod parts manufacturers, and custom shops had their personal T-shirts. The image of a hot rodder with a tight fitting, white T-shirt with Clay Smith or Barris printed across his back and a pack of cigarettes rolled up in the sleeve was practically a dress code. Only a small fraction of these shirts still exist as they were worn until they wore out and turned into cotton rags or thrown away. After all, why keep old, worn-out clothing?

Many reproductions of these shirts exist today. Bonneville T-shirts are prized; limited print shirts like Tony Nancy's and Tom Medley's roadster shirts are no longer in production but there are still original gems to be found.

In the past 10 years, techniques in silk screening have brought to market some fabulous T-shirts from printers like Andy's Tee's in Concord, California, owned by the famous "Rodfather" Andy Brizio.

New collectibles continue to appear almost daily. Chevron had a hot rod plaque that attached to the top of their gas pumps in 1995. After the promotion, many of these plaques found their way into the hands of hot rodders, then to the walls of hot rod shops and garages.

Many of these items are so offbeat that pricing them is difficult. Found at a swap meet, box art can range from 50¢ to $20. Products with logos, like Moon Header Paint, are $10 to $15. A Moon Tank runs $300 to $500. Moon scissors are $200. Posters are priced at $5 to $100, and T-shirts are 50¢ to $30.

Collecting pinstripers work is now an active collectible medium. Von Dutch pieces are prime but panels and striped objects from the Pinheads are now highly valued: Pinstripers panel license-plate size. Artist, Rod Powell.

This custom formed aluminum inset for a 1934 Ford grille is now mounted in the nose of the hot rod. Created, painted, and striped by Rod Powell. Hang it on the car or the wall, it s great art. Aluminum panel, 36 inches tall.

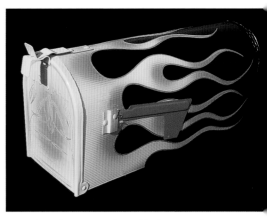

Flamed letterboxes are fun, and this hand-painted original can either collect the mail or grace a desk as decorative art. Standard U.S. Post Office mailbox. Artist, Rod Powell.

Original pinstripers toolboxes are rare, and this one owned by Rod Powell was done in the early 1950s when he was just a kid. Its angular artwork shows just how far pinstriping has come.

This Von Dutch original hand-engraved spray gun tank is rare and highly prized with its engraved flying eyeball and personalized top panel.

Art on objects like this paint can are part of the pinstriper s art form and this gorgeous 1-gallon can combines painting, airbrushing and pinstriping. Artist, Jess Hermosill.

There are a few ceramics out there worth collecting. This Stromberg mug from Vern Tardell in Santa Rosa is a cool piece for a drink or for storing pens or pencils.

Hey, it's Rat Fink! These 12-inch-high plaster Finks are hard to find but worth the hunt. They look great by the door or on the shelf, but remember to put them out of sight if the Termanix Man is around.

This original aerosol can of Moon Header Paint from the 1960s is extremely rare and possibly no longer EPA-approved.

These heavy-duty stainless steel Italian-made scissors from Moon were sold in the mid-1960s for about $40. They were great scissors, but expensive, so not many were made or sold. 12 inches.

Hot Rod Bicycle Accessory. This sound-making gadget attached to the bike frame and ran off the rear wheel, making the sound of an engine as the wheel turned. The same effect could be obtained with a couple of playing cards and a clothes peg. This boxed original was found at a swap meet in Long Beach.

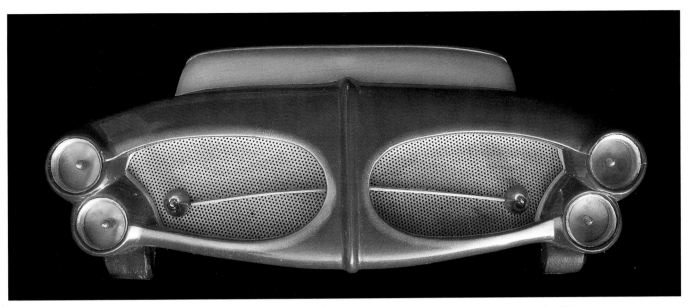

This original carved wooden wall art of Tony Cardoza's 1959 Chevy was created by C. W. Hale. Neat stuff and believed to be a one-off. Wood and paint, 15 inches, 1992.

The *Butt Wagon* ashtray was advertised in hot rodding magazines around 1952, but this "Jet Job" disappeared from the market fairly quickly. Rare, 5 inches.

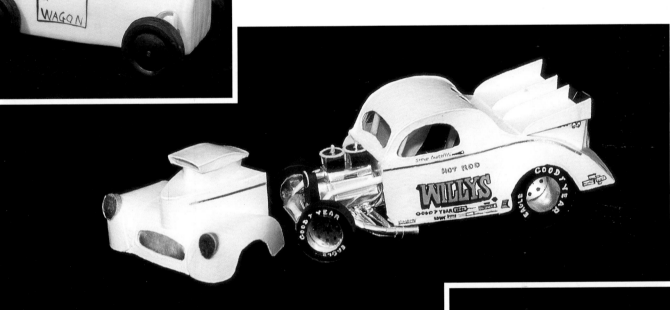

This model is a one-off made completely of paper. Created out of card and paper scraps by Willie Hightower, it is a near-perfect replica of Steve Castelli's *Hot Rod Willys*. Detailing includes lift-off nose, headers, and big-block engine. 5 inches, 1995.

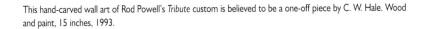

This hand-carved wall art of Rod Powell's *Tribute* custom is believed to be a one-off piece by C. W. Hale. Wood and paint, 15 inches, 1993.

This fiberglass *Jocko-liner* belongs to MoonEyes USA. It is a fiberglass replica of the *Moonliner* that Moon has used for promotion since the 1960s. 21 inches, 1992.

This is a fiberglass replica of the *Railton Special* streamliner raced by John Cobb at Bonneville in excess of 400 miles per hour. It is beautifully made as a collectible by Willie Chambers. Fiberglass, 30 inches, 1993.

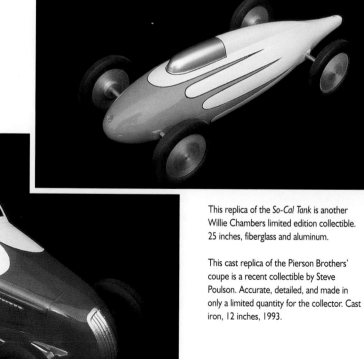

This replica of the *So-Cal Tank* is another Willie Chambers limited edition collectible. 25 inches, fiberglass and aluminum.

This cast replica of the Pierson Brothers' coupe is a recent collectible by Steve Poulson. Accurate, detailed, and made in only a limited quantity for the collector. Cast iron, 12 inches, 1993.

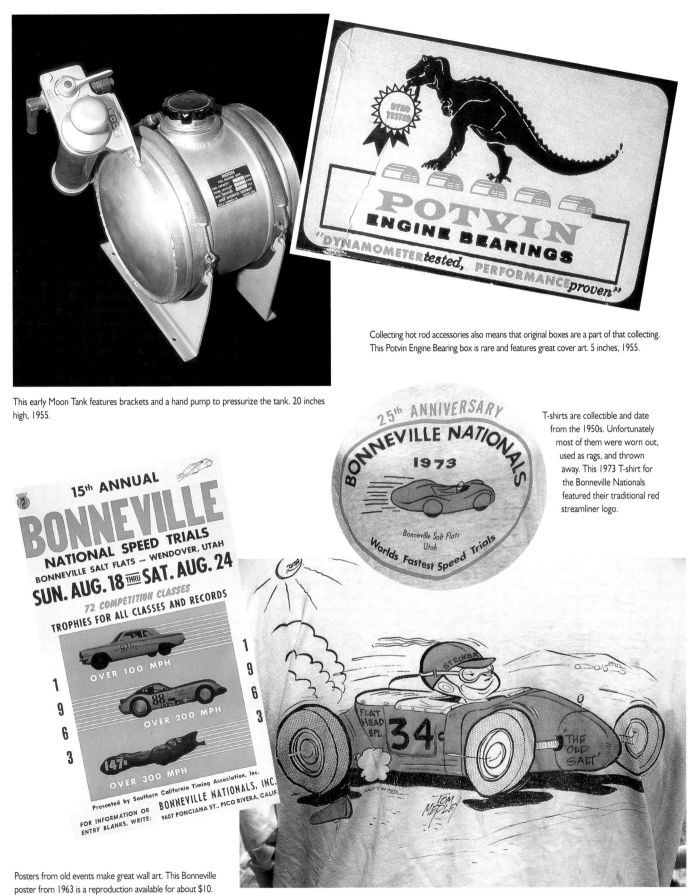

Collecting hot rod accessories also means that original boxes are a part of that collecting. This Potvin Engine Bearing box is rare and features great cover art. 5 inches, 1955.

This early Moon Tank features brackets and a hand pump to pressurize the tank. 20 inches high, 1955.

T-shirts are collectible and date from the 1950s. Unfortunately most of them were worn out, used as rags, and thrown away. This 1973 T-shirt for the Bonneville Nationals featured their traditional red streamliner logo.

Posters from old events make great wall art. This Bonneville poster from 1963 is a reproduction available for about $10. Approximately 24 inches, 1992.

Tom Medley's "The Old Salt" lakes roadster cartoon includes the famous Stroker McGirk. Printed by Andy's Tee's. 1976.

PRICE GUIDE

Toys

Prices for these toys vary enormously. "Used and enjoyed" obviously price differently to "boxed and mint." Kingsbury land speed cars from the 1930s go from $300 to $1,200. Sandbox toys from Buddy L and Nylint are $20 to $150. Renwal, Saunders and Nosco Plastics toys run from $25 to $120. Tootsietoy: Both scales price at $2 to $40. A new one is $3.99. Japanese tin toys from T-N Company, MS Toy, and Alps, etc., vary widely—1950s: $200 to $400; 1960s: $100 to $250; later: $20 and up. Aurora 1970s action toys range from $5 to $40. Small plastic cars from Hasbro and Ideal are $5 to $15. Collectible hot rods and land speed cars price at $120 to $600 and up.

Tether Cars

Pricing of these cars is extremely difficult. Complete mite cars run $350 and up, while full-size cars can price at $1,000 to $10,000; some extremely rare cars change hands at $25,000. The *Rodzy*, which is the most prevalent of all tether cars, sold for $19.95 in 1963 but today will bring up to $500 for a mint boxed version wrapped in brown paper. Swap meet prices start at about $80 and move up.

Model Kits

Collectors' pricing of kits is remarkable; an unassembled Ed Roth *Surfite* kit recently had an asking price of $1,500. Early wooden 30¢ kits may sell for $20 to $100. Special-interest 1950s kits run $300 to $600, while common kits range from $50 to $125. Rarer 1960s kits run in the $150 to $400 price range, 1970s and 1980s kits can be purchased from $15 to $300. The Giant Ts and '32s run from $80 to $250. Built-up kits in general are not so valuable but can command up to $150. Many early kits are being "re-popped" in limited numbers, much to some collectors chagrin but it has put some unobtainable kits back on the market in the $10 to $125 range.

Hot Wheels and Johnny Lightning Toys

Pricing is wildly wonderful. Collectors who know the hobby claim there are two prices for collectible Hot Wheels. California has one and the rest of the country has another. New Hot Wheels sell for 79¢ to 99¢ and the recent re-issues sell for $1.99 at local toy shops and drug stores. Used and abused examples of the early issues sell for $1 to $40. A perfect, in-the-pack first issue could sell for $250 or more. For detailed and accurate pricing refer to a Hot Wheels collectors' pricing guide.

Records

Pricing is dependent upon rarity, the condition of the cover, and the condition of the record. Prices start at $3 and run to $200. New compact discs are $12.95 through $19.95.

Books

Pricing for hardbacks varies widely. Book collectors are asking $25 to $40 for these issues while swap meet prices range from $10 to $25. Softbound Petersen *Annuals* run the same kind of pricing differential, starting in swap meets at $5 and going as high as $25. *Yearbooks*, especially the early ones, run $10 to $30, with the *Custom Yearbooks* trading hands as high as $40. East Coast prices are generally lower than the above West Coast prices.

Little Books

Pricing of these issues is always wide open. Early Fawcett books sell for $25 to $40 from dealers, depending upon their condition, yet can still be found in swap meets for $5 to $10. Expect to pay top dollar for the early Trend Inc. *Custom Cars (#101)*. It's worth every cent. Also expect to pay a similar price for Popular Mechanics' *Hot Rod Handbook*. *Hot Rod* magazine annuals command prices ranging from $25 to $40 for 1950s' editions and $5 to $10 for 1960s'. The Petersen's Spotlite series of little books varies, at some swap meets you will find them for $5 a copy while at others they might run $15 to $20.

Magazines

The low prices of magazines has made them easily obtainable to the collector and especially good value due to the added enjoyment of their content. Most early *Hot Rods* can be found for $10 to $25 although some early issues run as high as $100 to $200. The first issue of *Hot Rod* in fine shape can command up to $1,000. Other titles are more achievable with prices of $2 to $20. (The pricing of magazines on the East Coast is about half these figures.)

Programs and Catalogs
Pricing is comprehensive and varied depending upon the condition of the catalog. Inaugural show programs run as high as $150 while those from the later 1950s are $10 to $50. For a 1960s catalog the price is $10; for the 1970s, it ranges from $5 to $8; later ones are around $5. More common mid-1950s programs are roughly $25, late 1950s and early 1960s are $15 to $25, and 1970s and 1980s programs are $5 to $10.

Juvenile Literature
These books are inexpensive and are fun to collect. Trade paperbacks sell for $1 to $5 while old high school hardback editions of Felsen and others sell from $5 to $15. The Felsen Collectors' editions sold for about $35 new and can still be found for about that price.

Comics
The pricing of Charlton CDC *Hot Rod Comics* is hard to gauge but swap meet and dealer prices range from 50¢ to $15 depending upon vintage. First issues from Fawcett, Hillman and Ziff-Davis can draw prices of up to $75. Petersen Publishing's *CARtoons* runs from $1 to $5. Ed Roth's *Rat Fink* cartoon books price at $4 to $25 depending on their age.

Movie Posters
Pricing for posters varies with the movie and the poster's popularity. Insert and Half-Sheets are $50 to $200; One-Sheets are $100 to $400; Three-Sheets run between $250 and $600. Lobby cards are the best value at $10 to $40 if the card has hot rods on it. Movie scripts generally run from $20 to $250.

Early Advertising
The low cost of collecting ads is all part of the fun of hot rod collectibles. Laser copies allow collectors to assemble ads nondestructively and create a unique catalog of hot rod performance pioneers.

Trading Cards
It is difficult to price the cards. The biggest sector of trading card collecting is ball sports and some of these cards command enormous prices. Therefore the pricing of hot rod related cards pales by comparison.

However, expect to pay at least $100 for an unopened set of mint cards. A counter display box, complete, easily sells for $500. Single cards run $8 through $20. Single unopened *Hot Rod* Bubble Gum packs run up to $60.

Club Jackets
Pricing is select and personal and may well run $100 to $500 for a good 1960s jacket. Even higher prices have been paid for pristine special-interest jackets.

Club Plaques
Pricing of plaques varies in different parts of the country. There are many reproductions now being circulated and these are extremely difficult to tell from originals. In fact, a joke among collectors is that the way to tell an original from a reproduction is by its price, the original is cheaper! Originals range from $20 to $100, and reproductions sell for $20 to $40.

Decals
Pricing of decals found at swap meets and shows runs from $1 to $30. Some big-scale store window decals, such as the huge Dougs Headers' decals, featuring an orange 1940 Willys, can run as high as $100. However, average prices for small window decals are generally around $5.

Pins, Badges, and Dash Plaques
Collecting these items is relatively cheap. Pinbacks from the 1960s run from $5 to $25 with rare pins going for as much as $50. Embroidered patches go from $2 to $20 depending upon size and detailing, although some highly detailed dress patches can price as high as $50. Event hat pins run from $1 to $8, with rare items somewhat higher.

Awards
Prices vary widely for these items. Trophy heads command $5 to $25; complete trophies' prices are dependent upon who the recipient was, how famous the award is, and how badly it is wanted. The price can run from $10 to $200. Wall plaques are similarly priced. Old Russetta and SCTA timing plaque prices are not known, but expect to pay a premium for such unique items.

Miscellaneous Collectibles
Many of these items are so offbeat that pricing them is difficult. Found at a swap meet, box art can range from 50¢ to $20. Products with logos, like Moon Header Paint, are $10 to $15. A Moon Tank runs $300 to $500. Moon scissors are $200. Posters are priced at $5 to $100, and T-shirts are 50¢ to $30.

RESOURCES

Books

Barris, George and David Fetherston. *Barris Kustoms of the 1950s*. Motorbooks International, 1994.

Batchelor, Dean. *The American Hot Rod*. Motorbooks International, 1995.

Fetherston, David. *Heroes of Hot Rodding*. Motorbooks International, 1992.

Fetherston, David. *Moon Equipped*. Fetherston Publishing, 1995.

Gunnell, John. *Car Memorabilia Price Guide*. Krause Publications, 1996.

Gunnell, John. *Collectors Guide to Automobilia*. Krause Publications, 1994.

Holthusen, Peter. *The Land Speed Record*. Haynes, 1986.

Javna, John and Gordon. *60s!*. St. Martin's Press, 1988.

Mann, Dave and Ron Main. *Races, Chases & Crashes*. Motorbooks International, 1994.

O'Brien, Richard. *Collecting Toy Cars & Trucks*. Books Americana, 1994.

O'Brien, Richard. *The Story of American Toys*. Artabras, 1990.

Overstreet, Robert. *The Overstreet Comic Book Price Guide*. Avon Books, 1992.

Schaut, Jim and Nancy. *American Automobilia*. Wallace-Homestead, 1994.

Southard, Jr., Andy. *Hot Rods of the 1950s*. Motorbooks International, 1995.

Strauss, Michael Thomas. *Tomart's Price Guide to Hot Wheels*. Tomart Publications, 1993.

Tempest, Jack. *Post-War Tin Toys*. Wallace-Homestead, 1991.

Turpen, Carol. *Baby Boomer Toys and Collectibles*. Schiffer Publishing, 1993.

Wood, Jack. *Surf City-CD and Book*. Friedman/Fairfax, 1995.

Periodicals

Antique Toy Journal
Baby Boomer Collectibles
Car Craft
Car Toys
Custom Rodder
Gearhead
Goodguys Gazette
Honk

Hot Rod
Model Car Journal
Motor Trend
Mobilia
Rod and Custom
Street Rod Action
Street Rodder